ALL THAT JAZZ

All that Jazz

Learning to hear the kingdom tune in a new setting

Fred Drummond

Authentic

LONDON ● COLORADO SPRINGS ● HYDERABAD

13 12 11 10 09 08 07   9 8 7 6 5 4 3 2 1

First published 2007 by Authentic Media
9 Holdom Avenue, Bletchley, Milton Keynes, Bucks, MK1 1QR, UK
1820 Jet Stream Drive, Colorado Springs, CO 80921, USA
OM Authentic Media
Medchal Road, Jeedimetla Village, Secunderabad 500 055, A.P., India
www.authenticmedia.co.uk

Authentic Media is a division of Send the Light Ltd., a company
limited by guarantee (registered charity no. 270162)

British Library Cataloguing in Publication Data
A catalogue record for this book is available from the British Library

ISBN-13: 978-1-85078-733-4
ISBN-10: 1-85078-733-6

Cover Design by David Smart
Print Management by Adare Carwin
Printed and bound in Great Britain by J.H. Haynes & Co., Sparkford

Contents

Worship

Discipleship

Evangelism

Acknowledgements

Thanks to all who encouraged me in this work. To Fyfe in New Zealand, for all his comments and questions. Also thanks to June and Vanda for helping with the administration. I am really grateful to Lucy Atherton for all her editing skills and advice. The woman has the patience of a saint. To my new family at the Evangelical Alliance, thanks for your interest and care, and to Caroline and the boys for putting up with a real grump when things were not going right. To David Watson as an example of living out the tune. To all those who help make the adventure of faith anything but dull: keep playing the jazz.

Tuning up

I am using the metaphor of jazz as a basis to reflect upon
how the church may function in a rapidly changing social
climate. It is a call to revisit the way in which we live as
church and examine whether a lack of flexibility and
freedom is restricting us in fulfilling our calling as the
people of God: to be salt and light in the world. It is a call
to improvisation and risk, seeing change as a positive
rather than a negative.

I have tried to do the same with this book. Each section
is slightly different, which is reflected in the structure and
length. Some sections involve more story, while others
have more footnotes and take a little more time for
reflection. Section 1 offers an academic foundation and
draws different voices and opinions into the discussion
on leadership and its place within church and society.
The other three sections examine different aspects of our
Christian lives – worship, discipleship and evangelism –
and challenge us on how we can respond to the changing
cultural climate. There are also questions or 'short
intervals' in some sections and space for you to respond
to these at the end of the book.

In many ways there is more than one starting point to
this book. Feel free to fast-track sections and come back to
them later. Engage with the material in ways that are

appropriate to you. Improvise, have fun, take risks and play the kingdom tune.

You may enjoy some parts and disagree with others. That's fine. It's my prayer that this book makes you think about the huge possibilities that God has given us at this time. We are on the journey together.

Fred

Introduction

'Medicine to produce health has to examine disease, and music to create harmony, must investigate discord.'[1]

It is an interesting time to be a Christian. Christians are trying to navigate through very choppy waters. As we work our way through the waters the compass points that have served us well now appear meaningless.[2] For many of us this is an uncomfortable experience to go through. There are both external and internal factors that can leave us feeling cast adrift in a spiritual sea of uncertainty. Perhaps these pressures are most keenly felt by those within leadership positions in the church. The internal issues – those coming from within the church – include: falling numbers, the older generations with their declining energy, lack of finances and lack of personnel to allow the structure to function. There are more tasks that we feel unprepared for, and the expectation that we can cope and turn things around.

External pressures relate to the position that the church has within the perception of the wider community. We are moving from a place of shared hegemony to one of marginalization. Our status as a church is crumbling and our influence in the minds of the non-churched is diminishing daily. It is clear that we are enduring a large paradigm shift in the way in which we are viewed.

These are some of the characteristics of church life at the moment.

They may not all be bad for us. Uncertainty can have a focusing effect. Loss of things that we have always regarded as our right should make us reflect upon what is really vital to our faith. When dead wood is cleared we have more space for new shoots.

In this uncertainty Christians have to think about the future shape of the church. Various questions surface: Where is God leading us? What is our future? What might we have to let go of, to grasp the new things that God may be calling us into?

As we address these questions, let us not forget the resources and suggestions already available to us: from the purpose-driven church to mission-shaped church, and from seeker services to cell groups. These are to name but a few.

This book is not a model to follow but a journey to share. It is an invitation to reflect upon Christian faith and ministry in a different way. As mentioned in the preface, our travelling companion for the journey is jazz. While jazz is notoriously difficult to define it does contain harmony, rhythm and tone. Jazz includes improvisation and space. It is about careful planning and spontaneous creativity. It has a past and a future but lives in a creative moment. And it is a metaphor that has been used by others, particularly in the business world by Max De Pree[3] and others.

It is my belief that many of us do not function in these terms. We are more inclined towards order, control, management and programme. Yet these are the structures and thought patterns that are now failing us. Jazz is a very helpful metaphor to consider at this time in the church's life.

All that Jazz invites you to reflect on four areas of huge significance to our corporate life as church: leadership, worship, evangelism and discipleship. It is my hope that as we reflect together, something creative and new may be born that makes it easier for us to respond to what God is doing in our time.

Leadership

The rhythm of leadership

In his book *Gospel in a Pluralist Society* Lesslie Newbigin discusses the congregation as a hermeneutic of the gospel. Newbigin points to the central role that the church, as the body of Christ, has in pointing the world to the saving work of God found in Jesus Christ. The local Christian community in loving God, loving one another and loving the world is the signpost to the power and grace found in the gospel. The witness of the gospel will be found as the people of God worldwide live looking upwards to God, inwards to each other and outwards to the wider world. The church at its best is the best that the world is ever going to witness. Newbigin writes

> How is it possible that the gospel should be credible, that people should come to believe that the power which has the last word in human affairs is repre-sented by a man hanging on a cross? I am sugges-ting that the only answer, the only hermeneutic of the gospel, is a congregation of men and women who believe it and live by it . . . Jesus *did not write a book but formed a community*.[4]

God's plan for making the good news of salvation known throughout the whole world in all generations was to create and sustain a community of believing people. God chose to create and sustain the church. In this way the message is never 'disembodied' as Darrell Guder comments: 'The word must always become flesh, embodied in the life of the called community.'⁵ To see the significance of the church in the eternal plan of God is a hugely exciting thing.

Therefore the question that I am addressing is not whether the church will survive. Rather, it is what will the church be like in the coming generation? How must we change to facilitate the work of God in our age and beyond? An important part of the answer will be found in emerging leadership. How will the local church be led? Will the gifts required to lead the church in the future be a radically different set to what was required to lead the church throughout its earlier history? What will be the relationship between mission and pastoral care, church and culture in the lives of those whom God is calling to take his people forward? These are the type of leadership issues that need to be examined if we are going to take seriously the rapid changes taking place both within and beyond the Christian community.

Douglas John Hall in his book *The End of Christendom and the Future of Christianity* comments, 'To say that Christianity in the world at large is undergoing a major transition is to indulge in understatement. What is happening is nothing less than the winding down of a process that was inaugurated in the fourth century of the common era.'⁶ The term Christendom describes the situation when Christianity was the bed-mate of the State, the Imperial religion. Clearly something radical happened to the Christian movement in the fourth century during the time of the Emperor Constantine.⁷

Up until that point the Christian church lived in tension with the State. Though there was always a sense of anti-institutionalism and irritation between State and church, the extent of this tension was dependent upon various factors at work within the life of the Empire and its leaders. However, when Constantine adopted Christianity as the State religion the position of the church changed. To be a good citizen was to be a good Christian. To be part of the State was to be Christian and vice versa. This did not mean that there were no other religions still being practised. But the position of the church changed. It took on hegemonic influence. It became institutional in character. It moved from disestablished irritant to an established body marked by its ecclesiastical order and institutions.

Although a little simplistic, I still believe it is helpful to think in terms of the church moving from powerless (with regard to the politics and structures of the world) to an agent of influence and power. As Rodney Clapp writes, 'with the Constantinian shift the church decided to derive its significance through association with the identity and purposes of the state.'[8] This paradigm shift has influenced the western world for the last sixteen centuries. The church's institutions have been dominant. We have had a position of influence and control. The State and church have worked together to give shape and direction to the lives of its citizens, speaking with an accepted authority on all sorts of subjects. Clapp continues by quoting theologian John Howard Yoder: 'the most pertinent fact of the Constantinian shift was not that the Church was no longer persecuted but that the two visible realities of Church and world were fused. There was, in a sense, no longer anything to call world-state; economy, art, rhetoric superstition and war were all baptised.'[9] It is the church and State hand in hand controlling the lives of the citizens. It represents order, structure and control.

It is this Constantinian or Christendom model of church that Douglas John Hall believes, and I believe, has come to an end. The church as shepherd, power and authority within the culture has been eroded to the point of returning to disestablishment and marginalization. Hall believes that society has moved on in such a way that there is a rejection of models of authority and power. People are no longer looking to or listening for control or authority. It is true that the model of church which many of us grew up with, with its links to State hegemony, has been rejected. Therefore, the position of the church as an influence on the lives of citizens has greatly shifted: from the centre of society towards the edges.[10] I believe that Hall is correct in his assertion that Christendom is in a winding-down process of death. Let me give two examples of this change.

Come to the party

I grew up in a town called Dunfermline in Scotland. My family were good working-class people who regarded the family unit as vitally important. My parents thought that church was a good thing and were members of the local parish church, although not regular attendees. However, it was crucial for my parents to get all their children baptized. I had been very ill as a child but as soon as my health improved I was baptized. There would be something missing if I wasn't. I am not at this point considering the efficacy or validity of the baptism; rather that the baptism was seen as a cultural expectation. It was regarded as a rite of passage. It was important to have a baptismal certificate with the minister's signature and date on the back. This would have been the normal practice for the majority of families who lived on the same street as we did. Families and friends would come together; there would be the social gathering afterwards. It was a potent mix of religious institution and cultural expectation.

While as a minister I still get occasional calls from families with this expectation they have become less and less frequent. Indeed, it would be highly unusual now for those with little or no link with my congregation to make such an enquiry. We have moved so far in the last forty years that many people within my parish would not even think about baptism. They have found new rites of passage and new ways to celebrate.

Ain't no use complainin'

Recently the BBC decided to show a recording of *Jerry Springer – The Opera* on one of its channels. There were claims that material within the play was both offensive and blasphemous. Before the show was shown there were over 40,000 complaints. Most of these complaints came from individual Christians and Christian groups. All that these complaints appeared to do was to give extra publicity to the programme and those showing it. The unhappiness of thousands of Christians had no impact upon the decision to broadcast. The programme was shown as planned. What would have happened if a similar thing had taken place forty years ago? I am sure that more attention would have been given to the feelings of the Christian community, and that groups speaking on behalf of that community would have wielded much more influence. The church is moving from a position of central influence and authority within our society to a position of increasing marginalization.

In the introduction to *The Death of Christian Britain*, Callum Brown writes: 'This book is about the death of Christian Britain – the demise of the nation's core religious and moral identity. As historical changes go, this has been no lingering and drawn-out affair. It took several centuries (in what historians used to call the Dark Ages) to convert Britain to Christianity, but it has taken less than forty years for the country to forsake it.'[11]

Brown shows how in the early sixties a small split in the influence of the church on the lives of people in Britain very quickly became a large fissure. The religious framework to life that had almost been part of the psyche of society had been eroded and then rejected. Indeed, it will be common for many of us who engage pastorally with families in bereavements situations to find those with two or three generations who have had no meaningful contact with the church. The fissure has now grown so large that it is sweeping away many of the established church's most cherished roles and structures.

So what can be done? Concern and confusion within the church has led to many new questions for church leaders. These relate both to the internal structures of the church and to the desire to understand and engage with the cultures beyond the Christian community: our relational and missional engagement. What the church requires is for the leadership to plot a course through these pressures to find the new creation that God is calling us to be.

Internal issues

There are many people who have helped us see clearly the decline in membership of the church in the western world. For example, Eddie Gibbs and Ian Coffey in

Church Next spend several pages looking at the statistics of church attendance, particularly the United States and England. They write '. . . throughout Europe, Canada, Australia and New Zealand, church influence, membership and attendance have been in decline.' Later they quote George Carey preaching at the World Council of Churches Assembly when he said, 'In some sections of our western church we are bleeding to death.'[12] The point being that a decline both in numbers and in influence has been taking place for some time. A drip, drip effect that is draining the church.

If you are involved in the wider church you don't need a book to tell you about decline; you will be living with it on a day-to-day basis. The declining numbers is not in itself the real problem for leadership. The great pressure comes from seeking to manage a structure with reduced resources. Many of us are toiling under the weight of maintaining a model of church that can no longer be sustained. With less people to keep parts of the organization going we are forced to place more and more upon the faithful. We need elders, deacons, Sunday school teachers, worship leaders, but where are they to be found? A lack of penetration into the culture and lives of the younger generations means that the average age of the congregation is over forty. And so the church leaders are faced with an almost impossible dilemma: how to keep all the plates of outward life of this model of church spinning while resources, including finances, continue to dwindle.

Of course it is not all gloom. God is a God of grace and there are signs of his goodness throughout the church; miracles take place daily. However, for the majority of the time the leadership is involved in the draining task of managing decline. Many of those in leadership started off their ministry with a vision for mission. The mission was to mobilize the people of God to go into all the world and make disciples. However, it takes so much energy just to survive that there is little left for creative missional engagement. We have not found a credible way of closure both for ourselves and those we lead that might enable us to move on to a new chapter in the life of our congregations.

Gerald Arbuckle puts it this way: 'I believe we desperately need a spirituality that helps us to acknowledge the death of the once-powerful social status of the Churches in society, and the irrelevancy, even the injustice, of attitudes and structures that are obstacles to the contemporary proclamation of the Word of God.'[13] Arbuckle's argument is that we will not be able to move on until we have found a way of leading our people to an acceptance of closure.[14] We need to help people see that we live in a faith community that believes in death and resurrection. Yet to step into the possibilities of the new we must create spiritual and theological models that help us accept that the old has gone. Perhaps we would find a new sense of community and belonging if we could shed tears together and find the presence of God sustaining us in the midst of our sadness. Yet we find it difficult to accept that part of our growth must come through the pain of our loss. But that loss and sorrow may be God's way of leading us into joy. It is partly because of this lack of closure that leaders find themselves trapped into trying to sustain the unsustainable.

This can lead to discouragement and disappointment. Some leaders begin to question their own calling, while others wonder whether the decline they are experiencing is due to failings within their own spiritual make-up. Is it any wonder that so many people in leadership face burnout and breakdown?

External pressure

The congregation is the strategic witness to the work of the gospel within any local community. It is as the congregation faithfully lives out its calling in interface with the wider community that the gospel is incarnated: made known and understandable. We are the primary witnesses to the good news of the saving mission of God through Jesus Christ. As the Holy Spirit moulds the local congregation in its life and actions it becomes a living sacrament to the wider culture. It is the symbol of the grace and care of God. This authentic living missional engagement is our primary task. It is a hugely exciting thought that to be in leadership is to help a people live out God's plan as witnesses to his plan of redemption.

However, this desire for missional engagement can become a huge external pressure. How can we witness to the local cultures around us if we are not in a position to hear and understand the language and influences of these cultures? We need to spend time and energy engaging with those who live outside the local congregation. To be an incarnational witness requires a moving beyond the confines of ourselves.

But can we do this? This is the dilemma many of us face. We want to be relevant and we desire to hear what the wider community is saying but we don't have the time. To make the time would require a disengagement from some parts of the leadership role that we are expected to fulfil. Fulfilling the expectations of the church means spending ever greater amounts of time in administrative and organizational matters. This leads us to increasing disengagement with the very people we are called to be living witnesses amongst. With this disengagement comes a growing lack of understanding of changing issues and questions, and therefore we end up answering questions no one is asking.

The result? The local congregation has moved from incarnational witness, a relation-connected people, to an isolated and marginalized dinosaur. To live faithfully and communicate the gospel effectively it is essential that we acquire a constant awareness of the cultures that are around us. The way in which many people act and think is changing rapidly and this must have an impact upon the life and witness of the congregation.

I would like to highlight three areas of cultural and social change that the church has had difficulty in coming to terms with. Pluralism has had an impact upon church for a long time but many of us have failed to grasp its significance. Moral relativism and fragmentation, the other two, are part of the rapidly emerging postmodern culture. At this point I will simply outline these areas but they will also figure in the other sections of this book as our response to such cultural shifts is central to our discussion.

A trinity of change

A pluralistic society

In a previous generation if we were interested in a worldview, or sought to discover a pattern of moral guidelines or absolutes for our lives we had a fairly limited choice of options. If this worldview was to be religious then the options were even more limited. Many of us would have had to choose between different Christian denominations. Indeed in some smaller towns and villages there would have been almost no choice. The church was at the centre both geographically and socially. This situation has changed; we now live in a pluralistic society. Lesslie Newbigin is helpful here in distinguishing between cultural and religious pluralism:

> Cultural pluralism I take to be the attitude which welcomes the variety of different cultures and life-styles within one society and believes that this is an enrichment of human life . . . religious pluralism, on the other hand, is the belief that the differences between religions are not a matter of truth and falsehood, but of different perceptions of the one truth; that to speak of religious beliefs as true or false is inadmissible. Religious belief is a private matter. Each of us is entitled to have a faith of our own. This is religious pluralism, and it is a widely held opinion in contemporary British society.[15]

The religious options open to people within our society are wide and varied. There is a market place of calls, offers and free gifts of a spiritual kind, and the choice is down to you. There is no objective value placing one higher than another; there is only the package that you find most helpful. We are in a culture of competing systems and worldviews where adherents call others to embrace the system. The western world is full of countless religious communities and truth claims inviting us to become part of their clearly defined pathway. To embrace the claims is to identify your life with that worldview, to embrace that community. In this rapidly growing market place Christianity becomes only one option among many. The church no longer writes its message on a blank canvas but seeks a space on a wall already covered with various marks and messages calling for followers.

Seeking to share the message of Jesus in a pluralistic environment is not new to the church. In fact the church

was born into a pluralistic cultural context. When Paul
visited Athens we are told that he was greatly distressed
because the city was full of idols. The commentator
David Williams remarks that 'As Paul walked the streets
of Athens, on every side, in niches and on pedestals, in
temples and on street corners, his eye would have fallen
upon the works of great artists. But he saw their
representations, of gods and demigods not as objects of
beauty, but as examples of senseless idolatry.'[16] Paul was
used to ministering in both a literal and spiritual market
place. Indeed, part of his message was to leave other gods
behind and to trust in the crucified and risen Jesus. And
this has been the story throughout history. Those who
have been involved in the modern missionary movement
have had to reflect upon sharing their faith in pluralistic
environments.

In the western world some churches have taken this
market-place mentality seriously. They have either
engaged in creative dialogue with others, spending time
listening so that they can articulate faith claims clearly
and understandably in the midst of a myriad of other
faith claims and belief systems. An example of this may
be the success of the Alpha course. This course is a basic
introduction to Christianity and what it means to follow
Jesus Christ. It has been extremely successful, with large
numbers of people in the UK and beyond completing the
course. It has had a great impact both in the lives of
individuals and whole Christian congregations. Part of
the success of the course has been the marketing and
publicity campaign that has been used.

In *Selling Worship* Pete Ward writes

Alpha were particularly adept at publicity, display-
ing their endorsement from the new Archbishop of
Canterbury Rowan Williams alongside the latest

celebrity Christians . . . This kind of celebrity profile was added to a hitherto unprecedented financial investment in the advertising. Across the country, advertisements for Alpha could be found on buses, trains and billboards, as well as outside churches. As a result, it should have expected that Alpha would be widely known in Great Britain. The impact of such marketing was demonstrated by a MORI poll which found that 20 per cent of British adults could identify the course as Christian.[17]

Here is a group of people who have thought hard about how to capture the attention of spiritual seekers. They have recognized that we live in a pluralistic society and that part of this challenge is to make your voice heard. Most of us will not be in churches that can spend the amount of time or money that a national programme can invest. However, the point is that many of us still live in the belief that if people are spiritually searching they will naturally come to us, or will at least already understand why they should listen to the Jesus story. My contention is that this is because we are so caught up in maintaining where we are as a church that we have failed to reflect upon the ways in which society is moving on.

Moral relativism

The second cultural shift which has an impact on the church is that of moral relativism. I am aware that the term relativism is used differently by various people. I have found the comments and views in a book of essays entitled *Moral Relativism*, edited by Paul Moser and Thomas Carson, particularly helpful and insightful. 'I have always been a moral relativist' Gilbert Harman comments in one of the essays

As far back as I can remember thinking about it, it has seemed to me obvious that the dictates of morality arise from some sort of convention or understanding among people, that different people arrive at different understanding, and there are no basic demands that apply to everyone. For many, years this seemed so obvious to me that I assumed that it was everyone's instinctive view, at least everyone who gave the matter any thought 'in this day and age.'[18]

I recently watched the movie *Big Fish*. The movie centres upon the breakdown of the relationship between a father and a son and their ultimate reconciliation. The chasm between son and father revolved around the outlandish tales that the father would always tell. Fairy-tale like, his stories were of adventure, strange characters and wild situations. The son had heard these stories all his life; what he wanted was to know the truth. But what was the truth? Watching the movie, you are left wondering just that. It is clear that these stories were true to the father – it was the way he pictured his life. The question was whether his son could accept them.

Near the close of the movie there is a scene at the graveside of the father. Among those attending the funeral are some of the stranger characters that had appeared in the father's stories. Did their appearance validate the stories? Whose perception of truth had been correct or was correct even the right way to think about it? Were the different views and stories equally valid because it was someone's story? This is a beautiful movie and one that made me think about certainty, and the language we as Christians use in discussing the things that we are certain about.

But for many there is something unpalatable about those with moral absolutes. Those who are convinced that only their view can be correct are regarded as small-minded – or worse bigoted. Relativism, it may be argued leads to greater understanding and greater respect among differing view points and cultural groupings.

Gordon Graham in an essay 'Tolerance, Pluralism and Relativism' notes 'because relativism holds that unconditional truth cannot be ascribed to any one moral or political view, relativism in turn provides support for toleration; if no one belief or set of beliefs is superior to any other in terms of truth, all must be accorded equal respect.'[19] If there is no universal truth in ethics and no moral code has any special status, it is merely one among many codes; one has no right to tell another what they might or might not do, or to give value judgements on other moral or social codes. To do so is to show a lack respect for others.

Whilst western culture is becoming increasingly relativist, there are some issues such as child abuse that would be regarded as wrong by the majority of society. Yet the reality remains: we are living in a society where to elevate your views and beliefs above others is viewed with great suspicion.

Relativism is a huge challenge to those who believe that God has laid out clear guidelines both for the individual and the whole of creation. For those of us who have been used to issuing value judgements on others and decreeing rather than dialoguing we will have to overcome ever greater suspicion and isolation. How we relate to others becomes paramount to our internal and external existence.

Many of us are still shouting moral absolutes with a tonal quality of superiority that consigns us to a barrenness of real contact with a quickly changing social environment. How are we to counter this? The third area of social change that the church has to be aware of and reflect upon is fragmentation.

Fragmentation

By fragmentation I mean that many people within western society no longer see themselves as either having a purpose or belonging within any one group or community. Life is much more pick and mix; we live in incoherence and discontinuity. Where pluralism offers many options and calls to life, fragmentation is to fly like a butterfly without any particular route or end goal.

Jonathan Wilson, while discussing the relevance of the work of Alasdair MacIntyre for the church comments, 'In his analysis, Western culture is fragmented, not pluralistic. It is incoherent; our lives are lived piecemeal, not whole. The disagreements that we have are difficult to resolve because we cannot locate them within some coherent position or community. We do not live in a world of competing outlooks; we live in a world that has fallen apart.' Wilson goes on to write, 'we have moved from a time when our communities were relatively coherent and clear to a time when our traditions have become fragmented.'[20]

Life has no proper end or purpose, it lacks direction. I believe that fragmentation asks profound questions of the church: its life and witness, how we explain community, questions about commitment and discipleship, and the core question surrounding the purpose of our lives.

So how are we to respond? Do we squirm and squeal because things are no longer as they used to be? Can we really answer the external questions society is asking of us while we struggle with the internal pressures of decline, wondering where God is in the midst of this uncomfortable rootlessness that we feel?

Perhaps this rootlessness and place of wilderness is exactly where we have to be taken before our leadership can have an impact within the emerging situations that we face. Could it be that the Spirit is leading us into a place of loneliness and questioning, out of which we discover some answers, some more questions and greater faith?

Disappearing in the quicksand

You may have had conversations similar to the one I was involved in recently. I met an old friend for lunch. She has been in the leadership of a large church for many years. 'Everything is changing' she said, 'the congregation, its needs and even the way it views the leadership. It is a scary thing. We are not what we were, I am not sure what we are and goodness knows what we will become.'

I believe that what she was articulating was the beginning of liminality in her life and the life of the people that she was called to lead. If so, then she was right that it is a scary place to be.

I first became aware of the concept of liminality through the work of social anthropologist Victor Turner. In his book *On the Edge of the Bush: Anthropology as Experience* Turner points to ritual rites of passage. There is a period of suspension when individuals, or groups, are cut off from their old social order and structure and have yet to find a new identity: they are in the in-between place.[21] Consider a teenager who leaves a village as a child to go into the jungle, waiting to return as a man. He has left the boundaries, structure and status of a child behind him but he is yet to discover a new set. When he returns everything will have changed, his expectations and perceptions will be altered, as will the expectations and perceptions of the village at his return. His time in the jungle is a time between old and new, past and future, certainty and uncertainty. In some ways it is an image of birth, death and rebirth, or as Turner comments, pre-liminal, liminal and post-liminal. It is the place where you are free of past restraints and boundaries but have not adopted new ones.

While this may be a place of chaos and uncertainty it can also be the place of subversive creativity: the place to dream multilayered dreams using a huge palette, discovering new shades of meaning and living. To be in the place of liminality can open doors to fleeting glimpses of the previously considered impossible. In his book Turner calls liminality 'the release from normal constraints, making possible the deconstruction of the "uninteresting" constructions of common sense, the meaningfulness of ordinary life . . . it is the domain of the interesting or of the uncommon sense.'[22]

I believe that the concept of liminality is a very exciting one which can enhance our spiritual journey. It enables us to break free from the shackles of previous perceptions of church, faith and life: perceptions that we have found no longer sustaining. It opens up the opportunity for the dream and the vision to gain a place within who we are. But it is also a place of dread and confusion, where the certainties that have shaped us may dissolve in the light of a new consciousness. We may discover a new under-standing of our lives in the scope of God's redemptive love for the world.

Several Christians have considered liminality in connec-tion with the place of church within a rapidly changing situation. I have found Alan Roxburgh most helpful in his work *The Missionary Congregation, Leadership and Liminality*. In his book Roxburgh shows how Christians are moving into a place of marginalization. The old order that many of us have been used to is disintegrating. In this time of loss we find ourselves in a liminal state. It is, Roxburgh writes, 'a rich source of experiential maps that can suggest a way ahead for churches in framing a response to their changed social location.'[23] He goes on to say 'In comparison with its former social state, the liminal group is in an unstructured state. Old rules no longer apply; they simply will not work. Because of this fact, liminality becomes a place of undefined potential.'[24] For Roxburgh, the church that finds itself in-between is one that has the potential for transformation. At the time of his writing, churches were on the threshold of this liminal point. The temptation for some of us now is not to enter it. To ignore the massively changing place of church in society and the rapid changes taking place in that society. To sit tight and cling on to vestiges of the old ways or frantically search for the road back to a comfortable place. It may be that now these are not options available to us.

Exiles on the edge

One of the writers that I have found most exhilarating and challenging over the past few years has been Walter Brueggemann. While much of what he writes relates to studies in the Old Testament I have found that his work on prophetic imagination and the formation and reformation of faith communities have added to my reflections concerning liminality. It is in the uncertain moment that the prophetic is most clearly identifiable. When the structures that we have lived with are disintegrating then the chance to reform and re-imagine come to the fore. We are like exiles in a changing landscape. The question is, will we adapt and improvise or continue playing the same tune, centuries old?

Let me give you a flavour of what I mean. While discussing the exile Brueggemann writes, 'it is not necessary
or even preferable to engage in monolithic language, that
is language that is flat, too sure, too serious with too
much closure . . . whereas the Empire needs certitude,
exiles need space, room for manoeuvre, breathing opportunities that allow for negotiation, adjudication,
ambiguity and playfulness.'[25]

The ideas of space, chaos, ambiguity and playfulness
are all concepts which I believe have to be in the minds of
leaders living in a liminal time for themselves and the
church. They are about exploration and rhythm, themes
that I will pick up later in this section.

Whenever I read Brueggemann's work I am filled with
a sense of excitement. While the writing reflects upon the
people and theology of the Old Testament (prophet, exile
marginalization etc.), it is the language of the liminal. On
the theme of hope in the midst of apparent disappointment he states, 'The task of prophetic imagination and
ministry is to bring public expression those very hopes
and yearnings that have been denied so long and
suppressed so deeply that we no longer know they are
there. Hope, on the other, is an absurdity too embarrass-
ing to speak about, for it flies in the face of all those
claims we have been told are facts. Hope is the refusal to
accept the reading of reality which is the majority
opinion.'[26]

Brueggemann speaks of grief, longing, hope and
playfulness: of the new possibilities of the known, and the
dreams of the unknown, as people are forced to encounter
radical changes in their perceived and real identity. These
are radical changes from power to powerlessness, centre
to margins, hopeful to despairing. The challenge is to
create space to consider as yet unconsidered possibilities
that lead to a deeper dependence upon God.

A similar opportunity is given to every Christian today who is caught in the midst of the death of previous Christian ritual and boundary and is facing the future with fear and confusion. Maybe fear and confusion are the soil in which imagination, dream and hope grow. When feeling trapped by the pressure of maintaining a decaying structure and trying to offer certainty in a culture of uncertainty, the temptation would be to have no time for questioning or doubting – to lock away the thoughts and fears – but perhaps liminality is God's way of leading us into exciting new freedoms in our relationship with him. As the church's role and status is rapidly being altered within the wider society it could take us from fear into playfulness, leading to a new view of our relationship with God and the wonder of faith.

Short interval
- Do you think that the church can learn to improvise?

- In what areas of church life would improvisation make a real difference?

- What is holding the church back?

- What would we need to help us step out of the comfort zone to reach the lost?

Ain't misbehavin'

The main point that I am making is this: that as existing structures break down there is a chance to enter an uncertain, boundary-less place that enables new paradigms to emerge. Let me offer an illustration.

It was a winter's day in 2002, and I was studying at Columbia Theological Seminary in Atlanta, Georgia. My friend and I headed off into the centre of Atlanta to hit the malls in an effort to find something to take back to Scotland for our families. The city seemed strangely quiet. When we got to one of the malls the doors into the complex were open but there was no one there, not one person in sight. No security guards, no help desk, no customers. We wondered whether people had been taken away by aliens; or had the rapture come and we had been left behind? It was an unsettling feeling. We were both confused and unsure. Everything that we had expected and were used to had been removed.

When we got over our initial surprise we took a look around. All the shops were closed for the day, but for no apparent reason. We were the only people in the mall. Suddenly new possibilities came to mind. We could run along the whole length of the corridor shouting at the tops of our voices. We could ride the elevator from top to bottom and back again. We could sit cross-legged on the floor and pray for all those who worked and visited this centre. In fact, because there were none of the normal boundaries we could have done all sorts of things. We could have had fun, been creative, even risky. Of course we were none of these things, because we were continually drawn back to the uncertainty of the changed situation. We moved from the possibilities to the uncertainty and back again, until we somewhat sheepishly returned to the main street and discovered it was the beginning of the weekend set aside to remember Martin Luther King Jr.

As the certainties and normal boundaries had been changed we had the chance to imagine a different world: a new space was opened up for, the space of opportunity and possibility. Here was a chance for imagination and playfulness, the opportunities to rethink and see things from a different perspective. Ultimately, our confusion and need for answers drew us from that place (possibly because we are good Scottish Presbyterian modernists!). We weren't sure whether it was safe for us to be there, and so we left.

Things are radically changing for us as Christians in the western world today. Much of what has given us identity is being challenged. Old structures and positions of hegemony and influence that we have used as a comfort blanket are being snatched from us. Our praxis of faith requires reflection, not because we must take on the clothes of a new culture but because some of the 'faith clothes' we wear were inherited from a past culture.

For all of us this is a time of great challenge. For leaders it may seem like a place of despair as we seek to live between the 'what is and what might be.' But it is a time to imagine and reflect, to lead people through fear into new possibilities of being leaders and of being church. Do we have the courage to discover a new matrix by which to live as a faithful people in relationship with God and one another?

We regularly look back and review past church events or programmes, but how often does the church leadership look forward? And is that looking forward month by month, year by year, or do we have a long-term strategy for reaching the non-churched, for going out to the community as well as bringing them in? Do we have the courage to think beyond the box?

So where do we go from here? Now that we have delved into the current and complex position of the church in society, let's return to jazz.

Cryin' mood

Why jazz? Am I suggesting that we should all become jazz enthusiasts to be able to respond to the cultural climate? No, but what I am suggesting is that the metaphor of jazz is useful on a number of levels. First of all it is appropriate to a liminal space. I have briefly touched upon this already, but I would like us to consider it for several reasons. It is appropriate to a liminal space, meaning it has its roots in times of extreme marginalization and pain. It involves a fusion of various traditions and cultural forms, ultimately leading to new ones. Also, those involved in early jazz found themselves being thrust out of one culture situation into radically different ones. There is tragedy, pain excitement and creativity, as well as great uncertainty in the history of jazz. Let me give you some examples.

In the introduction to *Jazz for Dummies* we are told that change was sweeping through America, and people were having to come to terms with a new sense of who they were in the 1880s and 90s. It was in this time of uncertainty and shift that jazz emerged: 'waves of change swept America between the civil war and the turn of the century. . . . American cities wrestled with a new multi-cultural identity, New Orleans was accepting of ethnic diversity due to its roots as a French-ruled city. . . . The atmosphere was conducive to new combinations of culture and fresh forms of expression.'[27]

It is in this cultural stew of blues and work songs, African rhythms and European instruments that jazz began to emerge. It developed in an atmosphere of poverty, uncertainty and fluidity. This time of change was happening not just in the wider cultural patterns but in the lives of the musicians themselves. Jazz developed out of the sudden social and sometimes economic changes that were experienced by the musicians.

Louis Armstrong is an example of someone expressing personal change and uncertainty through his music.

His book, *In His Own Words*, talks about how he was marked out as a country boy, even though he had rarely visited the country – by his manners, his clothing and his naiveté. Huge changes were taking place in the way in which Armstrong was perceived and also how he saw the world. He faced new cultural experiences and a new set of questions.[28]

Jazz was born out of a time of great cultural and social change. It emerged out of sorrow, fear and hope. It developed as old patterns of life were being, sometimes unsuccessfully, challenged. That brew of the knowing and the unknowing, the experience and the challenges of a changing paradigm can all be felt in jazz music. But it can also be felt in the church today. As we have already considered, we live in a time of great uncertainty. It is a time when many of our old certainties are being challenged by new cultural questions. It may be a time of fear, sorrow and hope for all of us and it is a time into which the metaphor of jazz speaks.

The other reason that I believe that jazz is a helpful metaphor for us is that many of the main tenets of jazz are a good spring board for reflections about the Christian faith in our time, and it is these that I want to turn to now, firstly in connection with Christian leadership.

Think it through

Some people think that because improvisation plays a large part in jazz playing that little thought is given to the music beforehand. Somehow things just happen, almost magically, as people come together on stage without any rehearsal or thought. This is simply not the case, and we certainly couldn't base church leadership on this kind of thinking. A lot of thought, imagination and reflective interpretation takes place before the music even finds expression.

The jazz writer Gunther Schuller reflects on the whole subject of thought and the creative process in jazz, describing the idea that thought and work are not part of the creative process as fantasy: 'inspiration occurs precisely at the moment when the most complete mental and psychological choice for the given task (be it only the choice of the next note) has been achieved.'[29] It is Schuller's conviction that inspiration is essentially discovering the next step or the new move. This can only be done when we have worked through what all the possible next steps may be. It is the cognitive process of engaging, interpreting, reflecting and sometimes discarding that leads ultimately to finding that new moment.

Short interval

- How can we transfer this model to church leadership issues?

- Do we allow time and space for this at our meetings? Are we engaging with the real issues in our church meetings?

- Why are we sometimes afraid to discard? Is it the fear of something new and the safety of what we have known? Think back to Brueggemann's notion of the exile (see 'Exiles on the edge'), and the challenges that brings.

In the church today we need inspirational leadership. By that I mean that we need those who will seriously engage with the God-given tune of the narrative of salvation history and on our place in that story at this time. We need leaders who are not afraid to engage with that eternal tune and to allow it to shape us; those who are not afraid to sometimes discard interpretations and praxis that are no longer of value in order to find the next step. This takes time, thought and effort.

Jazz leadership then is about learning, listening and leaving. Leonard Sweet reflects upon the need for this. He writes about how in 1999 Panasonic did a special three-page advert called 'Leonardo da Vinci: The Art of Seeing.' It centred on da Vinci's philosophy, summed up in two words: *saper vedere*, or 'knowing how to see'.

> What the advertising blitz failed to tell its readers was that da Vinci painted no more than 30 paintings in his entire lifetime, and fewer than half of those have come down to us. Da Vinci was able to impact the course of history . . . not because of his powers of vision alone, but because his *saper vedere* philosophy presumed an ear to the ground, not life at the grindstone.[30]

The art of seeing what is not always clear is a vital ingredient of leadership today. To have our ear to the ground, detecting the way forward is a vital task. Sweet spends a lot of the book using the life of Ernest Shackleton, and the endurance expedition as an image of leadership. In a section entitled 'Lend an Ear' he connects listening, music and leadership in a way that I believe highlights Schuller's point about jazz and its relationship with spiritual leadership.

> To 'give ear' to anything – especially life – is to pay attention and learn. Attuned to the aural universe of

the Antarctic, he [Shackleton] listened to the soundscapes of nature, the vibrations in the air, the creaking of the ice, the voices of the animals. He could tell the world was different because it sounded different, and he studied the sounds to learn the difference.[31]

It appears that part of Shackleton's gift of leadership was the ability to listen and reflect upon what was happening around him: to become attuned to his environment in such a way that he saw the options and, having thought them through, moved forward. What does this say about the leadership required in our churches in this time?

We must be thoughtful concerning the environment in which we have been called to lead and be prepared by the surprising options that God may open up for us. This could lead into surprising valleys and unexpected mountains. Much of the order that we have lived by may disintegrate as we embrace – with courage – the cadences that we are faced with. Wouldn't it be sad if our leadership was marked by either an attempt to withdraw into the apparent security of the past or an unthinking desire to jump at a closed door? What would it mean for us to embrace new possibilities, and to be taken outside of our boxes and reflect upon the God-given possibilities that are emerging? In jazz terms it is to use all our cognitive and interpretive powers so that the next creative move may be recognized and embraced. This leads to exciting new steps for those willing to engage in the process. It is the challenge and the excitement of being a leader in today's community of faith.

The unending conversation

From Louis Armstrong to Miles Davis, Ella Fitzgerald to Wynton Marsalis, in every type of jazz from swing to be-bop, Latin to cool jazz, improvisation is central. Unlike any other music the need to improvise is the very heartbeat of jazz music. Of course this improvisation can take various forms as the tune is used as a spring board for jumps and turns in a whole lot of directions. Some may seem like a simple tweaking in marginally unexpected ways, while at other times it may seem as if the improviser has left the framework way behind and is playing outside of any recognizable forms.

There are many questions and factors then to consider. Questions such as: What is the original framework? What is the emotional intensity of the player? And who are the other musicians? These are all key to the direction that the music takes. The possibilities are almost limitless. Each time the musician plays they may take off in another direction – dependent upon the starting point, the way they feel and what the other musicians will bring to the mix. Each time the jazz musicians play there is the opportunity to play in a way that adds or takes away from what has been played in the past. There is the opportunity of constant fluidity of action and interaction.

In order for improvisation to take place there requires both courage and trust. Courage is needed in the form of risk-taking from the leader. It is always safer to give your own interpretation of the tune than to improvise with others and see what might take place. To improvise is to hold lightly to the platform or framework, and see what may emerge. It is also to trust and connect with those who are part of the improvisation. There may be new questions and styles that leave the player feeling distinctly uncomfortable. This calls for trust in those with whom you are playing.

How does all of this relate to church leadership today? I believe that it presents many exciting possibilities. To use picture language, many of us are comfortable with a conductor-led, orchestral style of leadership. The model is well-structured and requires a great deal of attention to detail. There is a huge amount of talent and energy involved, as well as a large amount of rehearsal time. The final outcome will be the attempt to unveil the conductor's interpretation of a piece of music.

There is nothing necessarily wrong with this type of leadership. As leaders we want to develop people's gifts and talents. We want those that we lead to see their potential and step out in faith. However, do we want them to take the tune into unknown places, or do we only want them to perform our interpretation of the music? Do we have a leadership style where we like to lift the spiritual baton and play the way we think it should sound, or do we share the music and develop together? Can we really claim to be leaders if we only want those who follow to play the tune how we want it played? In leading this way we may offer comfort to the players (we know how it should sound), but we take no risk and offer no adventure.

Improvisation in leadership must come down to creating a framework that allows for confident-shared communication; where the emerging, the creative and the spontaneous, are encouraged and where we are prepared to be changed together. Leaders will require openness to what the new possibilities in any given moment are. Perhaps the Spirit may direct us through unexpected people into uncharted areas that force us into difficult decisions. It calls for a change in style, a desire for dialogue rather than monologue.

Short interval

- What part does prayer play in opening us up to change?

- Would this be an important topic to discuss with others?

- What get-together would best facilitate this discussion on change?

- How could you provoke discussion within your church about the issues mentioned so far?

In an article for the magazine 'Organization Science' Michael H. Zack reflects upon how the metaphor of jazz can be used helpfully in connection with leadership in business. This reflection leads him to discuss improvisation as conversation. He writes, 'Ordinary conversation is pervasively improvisational. It is more interplay than dialogue, lodging people together in an intersubjective world in which participants mutually and iteratively create meaning out of interaction.'[32]

Zack goes on to make the point that spontaneous conversation continually throws up new directions and takes unexpected courses. It is 'unpredictable, emergent and [a] mutually constituted allocation of turn-taking, complete with interruptions, digressions, side-quips, non-verbal cues, and remarks made out of sequence.'[33]

At this time in the church's life it is this type of leadership that must emerge; one that creates and can live in the fluidity of improvisation – in conversation with God, the church and the culture in which we have been called to serve. It involves having a desire to play off those around us no matter where that may lead; having the faith to trust God and others, accepting that the goal is not my interpretation but our improvisation that will be key. Can we do that?

I've got rhythm

We have already asked whether we have got the time and energy required for this type of engagement. We can become so disheartened and loaded with disappointment that we pretty much give up. Sure, we still do the expected tasks of leadership, but that is all we do. Our passion and enthusiasm has drained away, leaving us in a place of dryness, and sometimes burn-out. Or, the other extreme is that we rush around putting out fires all the time. We hardly have a minute to think because we are so busy. There is something of this about many of us in leadership: we feel we must be seen to be busy all the time. We want to show that we work hard, expending energy for the sake of the kingdom. But this constant running to stand still can lead eventually to disillusionment.

Both of these problems are issues of rhythm. Getting our lives into a rhythm that allows us time to listen and reflect; space to simplify and to share. Leaders have to learn to live in a way that helps us to enjoy having a loving relationship with Jesus Christ.

Getting the right rhythm is central to jazz. Having a care for rhythm and its central place is what helps make a jazz artist. In *The History of Jazz* Ted Giola makes the point that part of the great influence of African culture upon jazz was the centrality of rhythm: 'The most prominent characteristic, the core element of African music is its extraordinary richness of rhythmic content. It is here one discovers the essence of African musical heritage, as well as the key to unlocking the mystery of its tremendous influence on so many disparate schools of twentieth-century western music.'[34]

Of course there are untold amounts of rhythms, and each can be played with richness and vitality. The important thing is to find the one that is most appropriate to playing the tune. As leaders should it not be the case that our lives are marked by the extraordinary richness of the rhythmic content of our lives?

For leaders in the time in which we are called to lead getting the spiritual rhythm correct will be essential, both to our own well-being and to those that we are called to lead. We may be forced to ask some hard questions of ourselves. Are we going so fast that we are out of step with God? Are we talking so much that we have lost the joy of listening? Has our desire to see the church grow become greater than our desire to know God?

As we reflect upon these questions it may mean losing some of the clutter from our lives to create that new pace. A leading American businessman wrote

> Complexity can become a distraction, though it is normal in organized life. By moving personally and organizationally towards restraint and simplicity we give ourselves a chance. It really comes down to setting priorities, as banal as that phrase has become. It comes down to dealing with the substantive before the superficial, of dealing with the strategic before the stressful, of leaving a legacy instead of accumulated assets.[35]

We must learn to make time in our lives for the things that have eternal substance: things such as stillness, beauty, laughter and hope. The most important thing will be creating space that allows us to grow in deeper communion with God. We must be able to lead because we are being led, and to share with others because we are learning to share in relationship with God.

Each of us has to find an appropriate pace, one that enables us to grow as people and to reflect upon the goodness of God. This may be different for different people and for various times in our lives, but it is crucial that we give serious thought to what is really important in our lives, and make space for them.

When discussing the theme of the sabbatical, Leonard Sweet highlights the need for slowing down, for what he calls 'MEGO' moments (My Eyes Glaze Over). These are essential to his own well-being, and he concludes that he is not very good at giving himself these times. He writes, 'I am learning to slow the flow and let MEGO. But I don't allow myself enough MEGO moments, and too often I don't allow others sufficient MEGO moments. Any member of the Sweet family can declare a spontaneous sabbatical that stops everyone in their tracks and brings the family to a common halt of inhaling God's holiness.'[36]

What we require is a halt to inhale God's holiness, a rhythm that allows for the joy of being. Jesus, for all the demands and expectations placed upon him, got up early and found a quiet place, a place of solitude. If it was important for Jesus to take time, think of how significant it would be in our own lives to live at the right pace.

Leadership in a rapidly changing church and culture will require the flexibility to improvise with others and create new directions. However, it is also important that the leader not only recognizes the correct rhythm for them but also mentors others concerning a proper rhythm for their lives. The proper pace will be set as we reflect upon what is important as a faith community. We might need the caring insight of others to help us realize that our sense of rhythm is all wrong.

Over the last few years I have tried to read the same book every year. I do so because every time I read it I am reminded of the need to check my rhythm. It is a book by Eugene Peterson called *The Gift*. In it Petersen discusses how the busyness of pastors and leaders can keep them from spending time on vital things, things that are central both to life and calling. Leaders like to be seen as busy people because it means that we are meeting expectations and showing others that we are needed. Early in the book Petersen makes this insightful and challenging comment:

> If I vainly crowd my day with conspicuous activity or let others fill my day with imperious demand, I don't have time to do my proper work, the work to which I have been called. How can I lead people into the quiet place beside still waters if I am in perpetual motion? How can a person life by faith and not by works if I have to juggle my schedule constantly to make everything fit into place?[37]

In the emerging church, leaders are going to have to find a proper rhythm for their lives in such a way that the community of faith begin to reflect upon the difference between temporal busyness and eternal significance.

Encore

We live in rapidly changing times. For those within the community of faith the changing situation can bring a great sense of unease. The temptation is to try and ignore the changes in relationship between church and wider society. We can keep doing what we have done, and how we have done it, no longer making any attempt to consider the implications of the incarnation on our life and witness. Jazz leadership recognizes the liminal moment in which we live. This may throw us from fear to dream and back again, but it is where God has placed us.

The call is to have the courage to believe that God is at work; to engage with that may mean radical ways of leading and living. Jazz leadership accepts and encourages improvisation: playing alongside others, allowing for new directions and emerging combinations to reshape who we all are. Leadership will not be about convincing others of your interpretation of the tune but engaging together to find new depths and ways of playing. The quality of our relationships will become key. Jazz leadership recognizes the need for a rhythm that enables us time to listen. The pace is not about busyness but about growth.

Jazz leadership seeks to develop conversation, constantly listening for the voice of the spirit. Jazz leadership will be misunderstood, criticised and sometimes treated with great suspicion. Ultimately, it will be leadership that sees following Jesus into the unknown as the calling.

I started this section with a quotation by Lesslie Newbigin. Let me finish this section with another quote from one of his books: 'The confidence proper to a Christian is not the confidence of one who claims possession of demonstrable and indubitable knowledge. It is the confidence of one who has heard and answered the call that comes from God through whom and for whom all things were made "follow me." '[38]

It is such confidence in God and others that will mark the leadership of the church which emerges in our generation.

Worship

The beat of worship

Like a great saxophone solo, or a clarinet taking the listener into a new place, the wind section of God (the Holy Spirit) did something unique and spectacular in the formation of the church. At the end of Acts chapter 2 we have a summary of what the church was like soon after its birth. They were devoted to the apostles teaching and to the fellowship. There was amazing excitement and a sense of awe; the apostles did miraculous things. There was a sense of sacrificial commitment: people were willing to sell their own possessions for the benefit of the brothers and sisters of faith. They praised God, prayed to God and ate together. They met daily in the temple courts and in homes. What a picture this is of the formal and informal, pastoral and missional, sacrifice and celebration. This must have bordered on the chaotic; it was certainly a continually changing environment as the tune of the kingdom was played out in the lives of God's people.

In his commentary of Acts John Stott summarizes this description of the church as a 'learning, loving, worshipping and evangelistic people.'[39] At the heart of this was the connectedness of the community. There was no separation between faith and life. The description is not of a bunch of self-serving individuals but of a people, together worshipping the Lord who had redeemed them. To me, it is important that no one is named at this point, no specifics of where people met, no details concerning the linguistics. The stress is on the corporate life of the worshipping community. They grew in faith, shared with one another and prayed together as one people. It was their corporate worship and life that gave them their identity. This is not a group of spiritual soloists showing off to an audience, but a people playing together in harmony. It must have been a messy spirituality, the messiness you get with life: new people coming, more to learn, questions to be asked, greater demands and needs.

This life was characterized by excitement and gratitude; God had called them to be his people and worshipping him as a people was central to who they were. They derived their identity from their Christ-centred, life-enhancing worship. They prayed together and ate together. They praised God and they sold possessions and gave as people had need. This radical, consistent living had an impact upon those in the wider community. Luke tells us that the church enjoyed the favour of all the people and that the Lord was adding to the numbers daily (Acts 2:42-47). This was impact living with worship of Jesus at its heart. No programmes, no campaigns but radical day-to-day living out of what it meant to be the people of Jesus. Adding new notes to life as others shared in living the kingdom tune.

What we are given is a four-fold soundtrack of the early church: it is Christ-centred, authentic, relevant and community-based. I want to look at these four areas in turn as we reflect upon the centrality of the worshipping community for the church of the present and the future for it is as the community worships Jesus that we find our identity and place. The account Luke gives is one where the foundations are known, but the structure is light. People play out the kingdom tune together in the midst of the messiness, and it is heard by others. We might call it jazz worship: a worship life that is based upon the foundations of our faith, but these foundations do not strait-jacket us into one expression. Rather, the foundations are so well known and have taken such strong root that they allow for improvisation and creativity. It is not a rejection of fundamentals; rather as musicians come together they have a trust and lightness of touch that enables new and exciting things to develop. As jazz musicians come together to form a common base that allows them to go in all sorts of unexpected and exhilarating directions, so Christians living on the foundation of Christ and living by his word can find that they are led into nuances that they never envisaged.

Christ-centred

There are many wonderful praise songs sung in worship services around the world today: lyrics that express the greatness of the Father, the saving work of Jesus and the anointing and illumination of the Holy Spirit. A great deal of modern praise has enhanced my own spiritual life as I have listened to Christian CDs in the car. However, I have also become aware of the amount of material that has 'I' rather than Jesus as the centre. Jesus is certainly there but is found at the periphery; at the centre is the worshipper. It becomes about what I need or give or want. Have a look at the index of any modern praise book and see how many songs begin with 'I'. Subtly a change in emphasis has taken place and my worship has moved from the awesome God and his amazing grace to my need and how God may meet it.

Of course we must be real and open towards the triune God who has called, redeemed and inspires us. It is only through the grace of God in Christ that we are able to worship and to come in humility and honesty. However, there is a difference between focusing upon God – and in doing so bringing our gratitude and needs before Him – and focusing upon our needs and then looking for God to act. I use this as an illustration of how easy it is for our worship to be impacted by the wider culture in damaging rather than positive ways. We live in a culture of the self. What do I get from this? How will this benefit me? I need my needs met. All of these questions may be valid in different arenas of our lives, but they are the wrong questions when we come together in worship. Whether the worship takes place in a house, a cathedral or a coffee bar doesn't matter; but it has to centred upon Christ. It is not what *I* get out of this but *who* it is that calls me to worship. It is to be lost in the privilege of relational engagement with the King of Kings.

When we place the emphasis on individualism within our worship I believe that we face three major dangers: the dangers of exalting ourselves too highly, losing sight of our salvation history, and failing to see Christ in others and ourselves.

Who is number one?

Our drive towards individualism within our worship requires me to continually be looking for God to be dealing with my perceived needs in ways that always remind me of how special I am. The paradigm shift from God-centred to self-centred gives the impression that there are two equally important beings addressing each other on level terms. This communication between two partners must be both lively and personal or one of the

partners (me) will lose interest – or will at least feel that
the other partner is not fulfilling their end of the bargain.
It is not enough for me to hear in Scripture that I am
loved and that God is utterly committed to me, I have to
feel it. God should bring me spiritual bunches of flowers
with my name and a note every day, just to reassure me
of his continuing devotion.

This drive to fulfil my individual need can lead to clear
dangers. It can result in what I call the slide into New Age
syncretism. I have been to two church conferences
recently. At both these conferences the delegates were
invited to take part in similar exercises. I was asked to
find a relaxing space in the room. I could sit or lie down,
or stand in a corner if I liked – whatever I found most
comfortable. Then I was invited to think about a garden,
and to picture it in my mind. What would be the size and
layout? Where would it be located? Now that I had the
garden clearly imprinted in my imagination I was asked
to think about myself in terms of a flower or plant in that
garden. What type of flower would I be? Would I be
thorny, would I have a scent? Where in the garden might
I be? Would there be other plants beside me or would I be
on my own?

After more questions and a time for silent reflection we
were encouraged to go for a walk and reflect upon what
God might be saying through this exercise. My first
reaction was that God was saying that to lie down on the
floor in a conference room is never good for your back!
My real concern was what type of God I was waiting to
hear from. Of course God can speak and direct people in
any way that he chooses. However, there had been no
mention of the character of God, no reading or reflection
on Scripture. Everything had been about me and how I
viewed my life, and then God was tagged on at the end. It
felt like a self-centred excrcise given a 'God varnish' to

make it acceptable. It also did away completely with any objectivity or point of reference. God has shown me what I am through my felt needs. It felt like an awareness of self and its development had replaced a desire to encounter the living God and to delight in bringing God glory.

While I believe that we must engage with wider culture and examine why and how we do church, still we make a huge mistake when we become the spiritual supermarket of spiritual needs. In discussing the Eucharist, Robert Webber comments that 'Unfortunately, the church tends to follow the narcissistic bent of culture and concentrate on self-interest or self-improvement courses. What can I get out of it dominates the choices we make. This market driven and consumer mentality that runs so much of church life misses the sheer inner joy Christians feel and express when they learn the message of redemption and reconciliation that is spoken and enacted at the table.'[40] By the constant drive for something new to experience we can allow our genuine need and desire for God to be replaced by the desire to feel something different: shallow superficial spiritual junkies in need of a latest fix rather than Christ-centred worshippers.

Find your place

The second danger when our worship overemphasizes the individual is that we lose the thread of salvation history. We are not just a random bunch of people brought together at this point in time. We have navigational points and anchors that remind us that we are part of a much bigger plan. When I first became a Christian I had a great problem with the genealogies in the Bible. I would skip the first seventeen verses of Matthew's

Gospel because they were just a bunch of names. Then someone took me aside and told me to reflect upon the way in which God had unveiled a plan. Piece by piece, life by life, generation by generation, God was at work connecting events and ideas so that his will might ultimately be done. We find our place in the salvation story only as we see our connection to those who have gone before and reflect upon those who may come after. We are a small piece in an eternal jigsaw. The piece is valuable because without it the picture is not complete. However, out of context the piece is of no value and makes little sense: it needs to be placed in the reality of the rest of the picture.

When we worship we must be reminded that we are part of the whole Christian community of all time and every generation. We have our connectedness through the life, death and resurrection of Jesus who holds us all together. This is one of the great mysteries of faith: that in some way we are linked to Paul, Peter, Luther, Calvin, Wesley, Whitfield, and every other believer. Through the work of God in history we have a commonality with all Christians of all time and it is important that we see our worship in that context. We are not divorced from what God is doing or has done, or will do.

When the writer to the Hebrews lists the great examples of faith in chapter 11, he highlights the amazing ways in which God has called, sustained and encouraged people – sometimes surprising people – to live as faithful followers of God. However, it is not just the names that are important. To the readers of the letter it is their connectedness *with* the people of faith that is vital. Whatever the readers are facing they do so as part of the heritage and family of faith. They are part of the people who have experienced great trial and sorrow but kept believing. It is because of that shared kindred relationship that the writer can urge them to action: 'Therefore, since we are surrounded by such a great cloud of witnesses, let us throw off everything that hinders and the sin that so easily entangles, and let us run with perseverance the race marked out for us' (Heb. 12:1).

In stressing the place of the individual in our worship and indeed in the whole of church life there is an ever-pervasive danger in losing the sense of connection with who we really are. The temptation is to see ourselves and our actions in isolation and to lose our sense of place and belonging. In focusing so much on ourselves we can forget the wonder of the hand that has been upon the church from the beginning. The Lord of history shares his story with us and we are part of it. However, it only makes sense when it remains his story and not ours.

One in the spirit

'All the believers were together and had everything in common' (Acts 2:44). While we will return to this in the next section I feel that it is important to highlight another danger in the stress away from Christ-centred to self-centred worship. That is the danger of failing to see both Christ in others and Christ in me as it affects the rest of the body of believers. The desire to have my needs met can preclude me from the fluidity and creativity that is at the heart of worship. Much of the way that God moves the people of faith forward in worship is through openness and love from the various parts of the body. To become self-absorbed is to be less open to what is happening in and through those who are around us. God uses the body of believers to grow, heal and change the different parts. Through shared story, prayer, the development of gifts and words of encouragement we grow together. But how is this possible if I no longer have an interest in God in others but am only interested in God for me?

The account in Acts that the believers were together and had everything in common was more than a geographical explanation. They weren't just all together because they met in a particular house or street. There was diversity, but more important there was uniformity. They had Christ and Christ had them. Their union with Christ meant that they were one people. I don't think they knew what that meant in detail. I don't think that they had it all worked out, but they knew that God had called them together. And it is as we recognize that at our core we are one with others – being fashioned together by Christ – that worship deepens and we see God's grace at work in millions of amazing ways. It is when we are willing to look and see Christ in a hundred faces that Christ gazes at us in a hundred different ways and we are struck by the greatness of community and our place in it to the glory of God.

To seek to cut ourselves off from the reality of corporate worship is to diminish what worship can be. Placing the emphasis on my need list is damaging to our spiritual health. It is not new. I once ministered in a church that had a large balcony area to meet the numbers of people who came to the church in bygone times. Now there was plenty of room downstairs for everyone who wanted to worship. However, every Sunday there would be one or two people who would sit up in the balcony area. They would sit long distances from each other, never even saying good morning. One day I visited one of the people who sat in the balcony and asked them why they didn't sit downstairs with the rest of the congregation. He told me, 'I like the fact that I can come in at the last minute, sit by myself without having to speak to anyone. As soon as the service is over, I can slip out and head for home.' He continued, 'I don't need others when I come to church; it is a place of peace, just for me.'

While there may be times when we all need a place of peace, to be part of the worshipping community is to focus our whole hearts together on the worship of the divine, lost in wonder at the love of God.

In our own church family we try to underline the importance of sharing our story together. Maybe it is a bit superficial but we have found it helpful. Most weeks we have at some point in the worship a gathering time. It is a time when we are encouraged to get out of our seats and chat to others. Sometimes there is a question on the screen, at other times it is simply a chat about life, faith and the talk of the week. It is sometimes tied in with a news slot, where people can let the rest of the church know about good and bad things that are happening in their lives. Then this can be used as a basis for celebration or prayer. It is an attempt to give space to reflect upon the ways in which God is shaping us all as we move together.

Short interval
- How else might we share our lives and stories with each other – both in the church service and outside?

My aim in this section has been to highlight a growing danger within worship. The danger is becoming more transparent as we move further into an individualistic and fragmented society. It is the temptation of displacing Christ from the centre of our worship and replacing him with self. Worship then becomes a thing that ticks my boxes and meets my needs rather than humble obedience and gratitude to the God who loves us. The focus of our worship should be the same as that of the great multitude in the book of Revelation

> After this I looked and there before me was a great multitude that no-one could count, from every nation, tribe, people and language, standing before the throne and in front of the Lamb. They were wearing white robes and were holding palm branches in their hands. And they cried out in a loud voice:

> > 'Salvation belongs to our God,
> > who sits on the throne,
> > and to the Lamb.'

> All the angels were standing round the throne and around the elders and the four living creatures. They fell down on their faces before the throne and worshipped God saying:

> > 'Amen!
> > Praise and glory
> > and wisdom and thanks and honour
> > and power and strength
> > be to our God for ever and ever
> > Amen!' (Rev. 7:9-12)

Authentic worship

Whilst our worship should be directed towards God it is also important that it is authentic. By authentic I mean that it is true to us as a worshipping community. It is our offering brought out of our real experience of being the

people of faith in this generation. For many Christian
communities today this will mean grieving, questioning
and honest doubting. As our paradigm has changed and
we feel powerless we should not ignore the questions but
bring them as part of the worship. The challenge is not to
ignore the cultural reality but to bring it to God, seeking
another reality in the eternal dimension of worship.

It is important that we see the connectedness of
worship and faith. Too often we have placed a huge
divide between what we engage in when we worship
and what we do for the rest of the week. We become a
chameleon community: changing colour and blending in
for an hour, then changing back again for the rest of the
week. Worship becomes a form of fleeing from all the
difficulties of life: hanging up any issues at the door
along with our coats, waiting to be picked up again when
we have to go back into the wild world.

Discussing the worshipping community Rodney Clapp
writes, 'Worship was an opportunity to escape politics,
business and conflict. Far from being a time of intense
engagement with the world, it was moved to a
"sanctuary". Far from it being an opportunity for people
to wrestle with the principalities and powers – to wage
the war of the lamb – worship was decided never to be
controversial, always to be comfortable and sentimental.'[41]

This form of worship, which we have all engaged in
from time to time, lacks authenticity because it has no
connection with the central experience of what it is to be
part of the Christian community on a day-to-day basis.
Rather than have everything in common it sometimes
appears as if we have nothing in common. To be an
authentic worshipping community we must focus upon
God with our whole lives. This may mean that at times
we are a grieving community, at times a mountain top
community, but it means that we are a real community.

And the community will always be fluid, changing constantly. Someone receives promotion at work, while another is anxious about a hospital visit. Someone who was praising yesterday may doubt today. Authentic worship is a messy spirituality. It involves relationship and engagement as well as vulnerability and pain. Yet as we come in our neediness we believe that God is able to meet us. Too often we have tried to be things that we are not. The temptation is to mimic another more successful community from a different culture setting. To live the kingdom tune in a form that is foreign to us is just as unauthentic as singing no tune at all.

Sing the song your own way

Billy Holiday was one of the all time great jazz singers. Her life was a turbulent one: from an impoverished childhood through to addictions to drugs and alcohol, and finally a tragically early death at the age of forty-four. Her life was the basis for the movie *Lady Sings the Blues* starring Diana Ross. While Billy did not have the widest range of voice or the clearest tone, what she brought to her music was a huge emotional intensity. It is as if her life is revealed to the world through her voice and her phrasing. There is an authenticity about her singing, it displays who she is.

Recently I went onto the official Billy Holiday website and looked at some of the things she said about her attitude to singing.[42] Here are some of them:

> I can't stand to sing the same song the same way two nights in succession, let alone two years or ten years. If you can then it ain't music, it's close or exercise or yodelling or something, but not music.
>
> If I am going to sing like someone else, then I don't need to sing at all.

I hate straight singing. I have to change a tune to my own way of doing it, it's all I know.

What is being expressed in these quotes is the recognition that you cannot separate the person from the song. To be true to herself she had to find ways of singing the song that were appropriate to her. Only if they were an extension of her could they be music to her. In the same way, I think that each community of faith is placed within a different culture, with different issues and concerns. Each local community unique. This uniqueness will be expressed in the worship that is authentic to the group. What it means to them to be united in Christ. It doesn't matter whether they meet in a cathedral, a café or a garden shed. It shouldn't matter how often they meet, or on what days. What matters is that they are encountering the living God together and in doing so they are finding that their level of faith and love are growing.

Short interval

- How is your church community showing genuine love and concern for one another?

- How is this expressed on a Sunday morning, or whatever day of the week you meet?

- How is it expressed the rest of the week?

- How can we move more towards the Acts 2:44 model of being together and having everything in common? Think practically how we might go about these things.

- How is your church showing genuine love and compassion for those outside of the community?

Authentic courage

What do we need to help a community grow in authenticity? Courage for starters. It will require investment in people and a trust in the grace of God. If we are seeking to enable people to worship with honesty and relevance then it requires a degree of vulnerability within the leading or worship. Can we create space for connection between God and his people? It can be easier to fill every second with activity because it means we are in control. It is safer to leave no gap in the programme. However, what about times for sharing and times of silence? Do we need to fill every second of our worship with words and song? What about allowing silence and space to lead us into the unknown or the unexpected? Do we do this?

Too often we have allowed worship to be a time of predictability and control, rather than a fluid mix of adoration, faith and growth. Each congregation comes to worship with the cultural pressures and life issues that help shape them as a unique body. Those with responsibility for preparing, planning and leading that body in worship must respectfully trust both God and the people. It is in this honest risk-taking that the transformation takes place. It is as we are given permission as the community to share the reality of our existence with God that we find God reshaping our reality. We are given a new perspective on life as we bring life – sometimes in all its ugliness and disappointment – to God.

God in mercy allows us to glimpse him in the midst and enables us as a people to gain new understanding of the context of our lives. Authentic worship enables us to gain the insights of the Kingdom of God: whispers of worth and value, status and hope. It allows us to see beyond our physicality into the eternal realities and

victory of Christ. We are constantly faced with images of
what the world views as success. We are bombarded with
the notion that success is tied up with possessions. We are
what we own, so we better own good stuff. It is what you
have, or drive or wear that determines whether you are
of any great worth in the world, after all!

Yet there will be those who are part of the Christian
community who, being faced with this cultural given,
feel failures. They cannot give their children the latest
things. Perhaps they struggle to survive day-to-day. They
aren't good-looking and don't have lots of friends.
Everything within the culture may scream at them that
they are nobodies. When they come as part of the
congregation to worship God they may feel deep failure
or disappointment. Yet as they worship, a glimpse of
another, greater reality comes upon this people. It is the
reality of the Kingdom of God and who they are in
Christ. It is counter-cultural; it is radical because it directs
them to the God reality that is theirs.

Worship enables the curtain to be pulled back,
allowing the light of Christ to shine through. Christ, who
came as a servant, had nowhere to lay his head but is
Lord of all. And so we are reminded of our worth and
status in him. We are connected to an eternal and
universal community, where not many are wise or of
great influence, but are called by Christ into union with
him. This union opens another world to God's people. It
is the world of hope and mercy; it is the recognition that
God is sovereign and that all true reality is found in him.
It is this encountering of another, truer reality which
draws praise and sighs of longing from the people of God
and enables them to deal better with the world that God
has placed them in.

It is in this honest place that the community is engaged
by the Word of God. In various ways the Word addresses

the people. Through teaching, but also reflection, meditation, discussion and dialogue, they are challenged and comforted by the Word of Life that is held out and shared amongst them. While I believe there will always be the place for the proclaimed, preached word, to have the courage to teach must be more than just that. People learn in different ways and to help the congregation grow we should keep in mind the diversity of forms of learning – ways that may be more challenging both to learner and teacher alike. 'Teaching' writes Parker Palmer, 'like any other human activity, emerges from ones inwardness. As I teach, I project the condition of my soul onto my students, my subject and our way of being together.'

Palmer goes on to reflect upon the vital part that teaching and learning play in our common growth: 'Teaching and learning are critical to our individual and collective survival and to the quality of our lives. The pace of change has us snarled in complexities, confusions, and conflicts that will diminish us, or do us in, if we do not enlarge our capacity to teach and to learn.'[43]

In authentic worship those who teach must be willing to become vulnerable. In the teaching we are sharing in three ways. We are sharing out of our own relationship with God (the condition of our soul), we are applying truth and we are allowing others to interpret and reflect upon how that truth impacts us at the intersection of our lives (our way of being). I find Palmer insightful when he talks about us being snarled by many things that lead to us being diminished as people. We often bring this sense of entrapment and confusion into our worship, and the sad thing is that sometimes we leave in the same condition. This should not be the case. Worship that starts with God and reflects the truth of God into the life of the community should be transforming. As we encounter the wonder of God we glimpse the reality of the otherness of the kingdom that enables us to live faithfully in the now.

Those leading or directing worship must feel that they can take the step of vulnerability and courage so that the whole community can move forward in their discovery of God. This may be a messy and sometimes frightening prospect which calls for creative honesty and scriptural integrity, but it will be worth it. In the culture in which many of us live, where the Christian community is seen and feels like a fringe minority, it is vital that our times together take on greater significance. Our worship refocuses our vision onto the God who calls us.

Relevant or counter-cultural?

At the time of writing, an article in one of the daily newspapers highlighted the way in which several congregations in the United States have used the words and music of the band U2 as a part of their Eucharist service.[44] The writer went on to comment about children dancing by the altar and worshippers seeing images on Plasma-screen televisions. Other congregations had been using everything from *The Simpsons* to *Lectio Divina*, or other forms of pre-enlightenment spiritual disciplines in order to find appropriate and relevant ways of reflecting upon faith and culture.

These are brave attempts to take seriously what influences people, and to think about how our faith can relate to the rest of life. I have been greatly encouraged and impressed by some of the creative work that is taking place within Christian communities. I believe that the God of the incarnation would want us to share and communicate in understandable ways. Jesus continually used illustrations that were well known by his listeners. He spoke in parables and took his images from the culture of his time. People understood about sheep, vines and coins.

Whether it was touching a leper, speaking to a Samaritan woman or teaching a crowd on a hillside, Jesus was always open and relevant. We must be the same. It is important that our worship does not become a closed sub-cultural event, where the language and thought patterns prevent both those new to faith and those seeking faith from participation. We must be aware of the culture into which God has placed us if we are to communicate effectively. Not to be aware of what and how things happen is a dereliction of our duty when we seek to bring the community of faith together in worship.

To ignore questions of cultural relevance with regard to our worship is also to ignore the possibilities of what God may be doing within the culture. Signs of his grace and mercy, illustrations of love and truth scattered around the wider cultural context, may be waiting for the church to discover them and to use and address them. Is God able to speak to the church through its wider cultural context? Do we need to reflect upon our use of language, style and creativity within our worship?

Short interval

- Pause. Spend some time in reflection now. It is easy to put it off for some other time. But the danger is that you will not remember. What has particularly challenged you?

How about the way in which we communicate Scripture? We must handle the Word rightly and faithfully, but we must also share it understandably. We must make the Word known. To make it known means that we do not speak into a vacuum, but to a group of people, and we must make it relevant to the group of people. The Word is too important for us to speak to people as if they had the same thought patterns and cultural issues as those who had just been through the Second World War. To be effective in leading and speaking will mean more time listening than speaking, reflecting than acting, and dialoguing than lecturing.

However, in addressing cultural relevance, let's not gloss over the dangers. The danger is that to be understood we take on so much of what the wider culture accepts that we lose our uniqueness as the church. It is possible for us to become perfectly understandable but have nothing worth saying anymore. It is possible for us to be successful, certainly in terms of numbers and finance, and yet at the same time lose the calling to be radically counter-cultural. It is not such a huge step to move from trying only to use understandable language to using only understandable ideas, and from there it is an even smaller step to using only acceptable ideas.

In a culture where popularity is based upon success and wealth, how tempting it would be for the church to omit sacrifice, cross-carrying and the exhortation to love our enemies from its teaching programme. Why not major only on the possibility that being a follower of Jesus will make you healthy, wealthy and wise? The grave temptation is to substitute ideas like judgment and mercy, and focus exclusively on love, which is a nice and multi-culturally accepted word precisely because it is so hard to define.

Louis J. Luzbetak, in a book about the church and its relationship to cultures, makes a helpful point concerning substitution: 'Substitution may be complete or it may be partial. As a rule, it is partial. Such is the case because innovations are generally unable to fill some or most of the functions that the original form has filled. In other words, new symbols, perhaps more often than not, do not perfectly coincide in meaning and value with old.'[45]

The church is a God-given counter to many of the things that take place in every other culture in all of time. In seeking to relate our faith and worship into any given culture we must make sure that we are not losing the meaning and identity of what it is to be church. Life is always much easier if we don't challenge anything. The problem is that to challenge nothing is to become irrelevant (the very thing we are striving against), and to no longer offer hope to those who seek rescue from the cultural givens that have controlled their lives.

It is a brave place to sit: seeking to speak with clarity and power into the culture that we have been placed in and yet to keep our distinctive voice. However, the danger of the mistakes should never prevent us from sitting in that place. To be faithful is to be obedient and to be understandable. In our drive to be understood we must always be vigilant in not substituting the foundations of our faith and therefore robbing the church of a central part of its mission – to be a clear alternative to any cultural group or society. The community of faith is unique and we should never dilute that in our engagement with the world.

Where are they all going to stand?

Returning to the Acts passage, one last point that I want to reflect upon is the way in which the Lord added to the number of believers on a daily basis. People were being continually added to the fellowship as the first Christians were noticed by the wider community (Acts 2:47). While I will address evangelism in a post-Christian culture in a later section, I do feel it is important to think about the link between worship and mission here. By this I do not mean seeker or evangelistic services – rather I believe that there is a natural link between how we worship and the impact that we have as believers in the world.

To focus on Christ in our worship is to see what is humanly impossible become possible. As we humble ourselves, we see that our own weakness and frailty are not the full stop at the end of the sentences that are our lives. Rather, God opens up a whole new chapter of uncharted possibilities: kingdom possibilities that may transform our world. Through worship we can see a new reality, one based upon God's sovereign power. We then go back into the family situation and the work place, able to live as authentic Christians. To be who we are in Christ with confidence makes us natural channels of love and grace.

If our worship is open, relevant and clear then we are being equipped to live out our faith in the world. I believe that to do this our worship must celebrate our uniqueness in Christ. Not only in what we do in the church but in whom we are in God. We must praise and thank God for where he has placed us: where we work, the street we live in, the difficulties we go through. The whole of our journey should be important to the whole Christian community, as it is important to the Saviour. That is one of the things that make the worshipping community such a fluid and exciting thing: that we are one and also unique: that we live out our lives in the world and yet together in Christ. This should lead us to a place of vulnerability and honesty, but also to a position of sharing burdens and praying and encouraging each other. The challenge is to see our whole lives from that worshipping community perspective so that when we are away from the body, the body is still with us and through Christ helping us to deal with the adventure of living in the world.

Our worship makes us naturally missional because we simply want to live our lives authentically. This is not a programme or even a set of well-rehearsed verses, but honest living with Jesus that enables us to have honest encounters with the world. In a world where speed and superficiality have become the norm, we will find that reliable relationships are what people earnestly crave. Our worship can help us have the type of character that enables us to develop such relationships. People in the wider community look on and notice how we live our lives. It is living faithfully in these places – the difficult places – that God uses to advance the kingdom.

Short interval

- How can we make ourselves available to the wider community?

- Are people being added to our local church? If not, why not? How are you involved in local outreach and evangelism – in your work place, the home, and in your free time?

- How can we counter the danger of becoming spiritual hermits?

So what steps can be taken? Believers must think about the outsider coming in. If they invited non-Christians to their church service would they feel embarrassed by what takes place? Or would they find that the message was accessible, relevant and challenging?

I have met several believers who have revealed that they would not invite people to their church because they would be embarrassed by how their friends might view what took place. They were not demanding some great overhaul, just for the services to be more understandable.

An elderly choir, an exclusive language, a long talk with little to tie it to the real world. I know that I am painting a worst case scenario (or not), but one which will be the shared experience of many. It is often worship packed with assumptions about the knowledge of those who gather.

An example of this was found in the early days of Perth Riverside when we worshipped in a school. Sometimes as part of the service we would have a small group question that encouraged discussion. Normally the questions were open, easy questions that were addressed in the sermon. One Sunday we were beginning a series on the parables and I asked people to discuss their favourite. What an idiot I was. We had folks chatting about the Christmas story, Easter, and even Adam and Eve. Many people who had attended did not know what a parable was. And my use of language had been exclusive instead of inclusive. I should have given some thought to what I meant by parable and how I could explain that in our ministry context.

Imagine if someone had prayed and invited a friend to church who had no experience of faith and no knowledge of church, and was thrust into this culture that he did not understand; where there had been no attempt made to include them. Imagine when we all began to recite the Lord's Prayer and everybody said the words except them, because they didn't know them. Picture the Christian who has talked about Jesus and his love and grace, but who is unsure whether such love and grace would be witnessed by a stranger in their own congregation. Worship – authentic, real and Christ-centred – enables the believer to live missionally both in the world and in the church.

Reprise

In this section I have tried to think about worship in the post-Christian era. My contention is that we have moved into a new time in the life of the church. It is a time of less influence: a period where to be part of the Christian community is to be a minority whose views carry little weight in the wider culture setting. In this respect it has been helpful to reflect upon the account of the early church in the book of Acts to look at what was important to that marginalized community. For it is as we come together and share our lives in Christ that we find meaning and belonging. It is when we focus upon Christ in word and sacrament that we discover the greater reality of the Kingdom of God. This in turn equips us to live in the world in such a way that we make a difference; living for the glory of God.

This makes worship naturally relational and missional. We grow in relationship with one another and with the Lord who calls us, and we also have the confidence to build relationships with those who are not part of the community of faith. The key to building this relational and missional worship is the desire to be both Christ-centred and creative. We need people who lead our worship, in whatever form that might take to be bold, understanding both the Word and the world. We must set a course between the individuality of our day and the legalism of our past. Risk taking, truth and encouragement come together as the Christian community seeks to live out its uniqueness in a postmodern, secular environment. It is honest, authentic devotion to Jesus and to one another, highlighted in the worship that will act as a counter to the accepted ideas of the wider culture. We need the freedom and improvisation to respond to our God, and to the situation that he has placed us in. As we respond to God and to our family of faith we should find we are developing at the same time – developing as a group as we individually enhance and strengthen the whole.

As I write this I am listening to a recording of Louis Armstrong and Duke Ellington from their album called 'The Great Summit: The Master Takes.' They are two hugely individual players who bring something of themselves to their art, and here on this recording they play together. As they do so they appear to lift each other to new heights. As the trumpet (Armstrong) and the piano (Ellington) respond to each other the fusion lifts the music to new levels without ever diminishing the extraordinary ability of each. This helps me to reflect upon worship. Christ is at the centre of our worship. We focus on him and on the glory of God. As we do, we come together as a community, bringing who we are and what we are becoming into the light of his presence.

Amazing things happen. Our focus is realigned to the alternative kingdom and we are drawn to God and to each other. Improvisation and growth take place, sometimes in the most unexpected ways. In all of this we are never diminished but rather we are challenged to greater kingdom living in the world. Our corporate worship takes us to new levels of hope in Christ and enables us to live more effectively for God. My worship with others at greater and greater levels of vulnerability and creativity enhances who I am in Christ.

Short interval
- Is my worship focused upon God or myself?

- Does my worship help me to live more faithfully in the world?

- What are the signs of growing love and grace within my worshipping community?

- In what ways do we care for the stranger who comes amongst us?

Worship – key notes

There was ten minutes left at the end of the lecture. I had said all I wanted to say. The theme had been 'Postmodern Worship and Evangelism'. I was to give four two-hour sessions. Having nothing else to say that would have been worth hearing I asked for any questions. She put her hand up straight away. I guess she was in her late twenties; she looked studious, and I thought I was going to be challenged on some point I had made, which is always fun.

'I found your analysis and challenge to be really helpful and encouraging.'

I liked her already.

She continued, 'But we need more than that. What are your springboards? What are the images and ideas that you started with that have led to the way you talk and think about church? We need some jumping off places so that we can think in different ways. Can you share the launch pad things that get your mind working out of the box? I think that would be the most helpful thing for me.'

I wasn't sure whether that meant that everything else that I had said was not that helpful, but it did make me think. On speaking to several of my friends I've got a similar response: It is important to get the detail of where the church is and what is happening to it, but wouldn't it be great if there were some basic ideas out there that could be turned in any direction? I guess that is a little of what jazz is, a few starting notes from which to go in lots of different directions. There have been a whole lot of starting notes for me and I am grateful to the people whose insights have inspired me to think in new ways. Here, I will try to share a few of these notes and where they have taken me in my thinking about worship and the worshipping community. My hope is not that you will agree, or find that you are playing the same tune, but that these notes might lead you to exciting variations.

Rehearsing

I first came across the idea of worship as rehearsal from Robert Webber. He makes clear that he uses the idea in terms of fluid relationship or fluid motion between God and the worshipper.

> Worship is a dialogue between the divine action and human response. It rehearses the relationship between God and man as it is done. As we worship we are opening our lives afresh to an interaction with God through immersion in the kingdom story. . . . This interaction between the worshiper and God rehearses our relationship as it is lived out in the world. This kind of worship is not designed to be an entertaining programme, or a rational presentation. . . . Instead, in its simple and authentic way, the dialogue that takes place in worship between God and the worshiper invites the worshiper to enter into a relationship with God.[46]

The worship is something wonderful in itself but it also prepares me for my relationship with God in the world.

The idea of rehearsal also makes me think about the eternal context of our worship. While what we do as the community of faith is real and transforming through the grace of God, it is also part of a universal and eternal worship. My human base may be Perth in Scotland, but my worship is much bigger and more significant than that. It is part of the tapestry of worship coming to God from every tribe, tongue and nation. Our worship fits uniquely into the whole realm of worship from around the globe. Without our worship there is something missing from all that God deserves.

While we may not know or understand the worship of others still we have a connection with something more wonderful than we can imagine. As we gather in our diversity we point to a greater diversity within the wider worshipping community. As we laugh or cry we point to laughter and tears, perhaps of greater intensity in other parts of the universal community. In our praise, prayers, preaching and sharing we are rehearsing what is taking place in different forms and times throughout the world, and adding our own flavour to the universal dish of worship. And this dish in itself points to an ultimate fulfilment when the eternal worshipping community come face to face with God.

> Then I heard what sounded like a great multitude,
> like the roar of rushing waters and like loud peals of
> thunder, shouting:
> 'Hallelujah!
> For our Lord God Almighty reigns.
> Let us rejoice and be glad
> and give him glory!
> For the wedding of the Lamb has come,
> and his bride has made herself ready.
> Fine linen, bright and clean,
> was given her to wear.'

... Then the angel said to me, 'Write: "Blessed are those who are invited to the wedding supper of the Lamb!"' (Rev. 19:6-9)

This is worship that is unrestricted, where pain, sorrow and death no longer hold us back from the ultimate expression of our union with God in Christ.

Short interval
- Reflect for 5-10 minutes. How does being part of the universal church and our ultimate eternal worship impact what we do together?

Leaver-sensitive worship

As soon as I heard this term it really began to make me think about those who are not seeking, but leaving. There are those who no longer find that the corporate worship is sustaining their walk with God. And the number of people who are turning their backs on organized worship of any kind is growing. This is not necessarily done in anger but in disappointment and discouragement. I am thinking of people with a genuine faith and a desire to live out that faith in the world who no longer see church (primarily meaning corporate worship and support) as being relevant to them. I have heard it argued that this is solely a symptom of the culture of individualism, and a rejection of accountability, and we should not pander to it in any way. While I do think that there are cultural issues involved in those who walk away, I feel that there are also spiritual ones that we as a church need to reflect upon in our worship.

A Churchless Faith by Alan Jamieson charts the spiritual journey of some of those who have moved out from, or beyond the churches. As I read the book, two things struck me in particular about those who are in the process of leaving church or have already decided that organized church is no longer for them. They are the group that Jamieson calls 'reflective exiles'.[47] Firstly, there is the fact that some people find building relationships much more difficult than others. Or they reject the forms of relationship building that the church normally employs. Here is a challenge for us all. While we may believe that church is by its nature relational how much time and space do we give to those who find this difficult? Do we neglect to give much time because we find it hard work?

I have a friend who moved to a new town and was looking for a church to be part of. He had visited a well-known church the day before I phoned him. I asked him about it.

'How was the worship?'

'Really good' he replied. 'It was very thoughtful and extremely well done.'

'Do you think that you will go back?'

'Definitely not, I was left with no exit strategy.'

He went on to explain that as he entered the church he was accosted by a woman who wanted to give him a welcome hug. Then, at the conclusion of the praise he was escorted into a lounge for coffee. My friend is quiet and shy. What he wanted was to find a spiritual space, and in his own time to connect with people. Maybe a drop-in or discussion group where he could participate in if he felt comfortable. My friend has a real and genuine faith but is struggling with church. I believe that church is relational but I am challenged about how I can make space for people like him.

Recently in our church we asked people to write down themes that they would like to be addressed in our church service. These could be issues that concerned them or subjects that they didn't think were talked about in the church. We put up a large flip chart for people to write their ideas on and I promised that we would try and tackle as many as we could over the next few months. What was written down came as a surprise. The one that topped the bill was self-image. Several people also wrote 'Is it OK to be angry with God?' There were questions on forgiveness and worth. 'How to keep faith in the midst of an unbelieving world' was also high on the agenda. These were real issues that related to people's everyday existence as they sought to follow Jesus in the world.

As we tried to discuss these topics it was clear that simply teaching through them was not going to be enough. So we decided to create space for people to talk and reflect. Sometimes we started with an opener for discussion in small groups; this was then followed up later in the service. On other occasions we had quiet places where worshippers could take time out and reflect. We were attempting to incorporate the need in some to retreat and reflect, making space for those on the margins; the 'reflective exiles' as Jamieson calls them.

Short interval

- How many people have drifted away from your fellowship in the last two years?

- Why did they leave?

- What attempts were made to find out about their difficulties?

- Has their leaving made you change anything that you do in worship?

Community-based

Opening the curtains

It is early morning and the room is dark. It is hard to see what is close to you. As you get up you try and focus upon where things are. You head timidly towards the windows. Stumbling over a shoe and then bashing your toe against something you try and tread carefully. As if picking your way through a minefield at last you reach your destination. With a flourish you pull back the curtains and summer sunlight floods into the room. Suddenly all becomes clear and you can see exactly what it was that you fell over. As you gaze out of the window your attention is taken from the room itself to what is outside, things that you were unaware of while the curtains were closed. In an instance your whole perspective changes.

I sometimes think about worship as the time when we open the curtains and get a new view, where things are suddenly put into focus. I have found this to be a useful image in three different ways.

When we come to worship and open our hearts to the work of the Spirit we are allowed, by grace, to glimpse something of the greatness and glory of God. It is as if the curtain has been pulled back and we glimpse a new world. It is an unexpected one full of wonder and unanswered questions. Like Lucy as she stepped from the wardrobe into the unknown, so we are invited into a new dimension of how life can be.

It was as Lucy went through the wardrobe that she stepped into a reality that she could not access in any other way. As she encountered the unexpected she was challenged to think in new ways. Many things that she had taken for granted were now less certain because of the new world that she had encountered.

Worship should do that for us. It should offer glimpses of a deeper reality that forces us to think in new ways. It helps put the things of the immediate into a proper perspective, and while it can be frightening it is ultimately reassuring because it lets us see the glory of the King and his Kingdom breaking into our tired existence.

Of course there is another side to opening the curtains and allowing the light in, and this is my second point. Not only do we get a new view beyond, we also see more clearly the dust and dirt that lie within. Worship must challenge us by exposing who we are and what we are doing. I see this as a prophetic edge to our worship. By this I don't mean that we have predictions about the future or nice pictures to cheer us. I believe that there must be an element in our worship that forces us to ask whether we love justice and seek mercy. Worship should force us to confront our attitudes about the widow and orphan. Worship should challenge us about our wealth and our lifestyle choices, about attitudes to brothers and sisters facing difficulties in other parts of the world. Our engagement in worship should make us ponder the gift of creation and how we are caring for such a wonderful gift.

Thirdly, worship should be asking serious questions about whether our corporate and individual lives are being lived in accordance with God's call or the call of the cultures that surround us. We need to be reminded that we are a unique people, a universal family that is characterized by our likeness of and obedience to the Lord. Worship must challenge us to the distinctiveness of our calling, no matter how painful that may be for us.

In worship we need to open the curtain to allow both encouragement and challenge.

> **Short interval**
> • How does your worship intentionally challenge the attitudes of the worshipping community?
>
> • How can you review the impact that worship is having in forming radical love?

Two types of people

I attended a conference recently which was led by Mark Greene. During the conference the church was being encouraged to pray for and support people in their daily work. How hard it is to be the only Christian in the staff room or in the college year group. It is not easy to try and live out faith in an environment which totally disregards what you have to say. The local church, in the main service of worship, calls upon teachers, plumbers or whoever else, and asks them to stand and be confirmed in their work. I believe this is hugely important. It is not easy to live out faith in our generation, and so we must support each other in our work within the wider society. The greatest temptation is to simply assimilate into the culture, not stand against it. It is much easier not to ask questions, not to make people uncomfortable by what we think.

> **Short interval**
> • Think back to the 'Exiles on the edge' section where we considered Walter Brueggemann's work, and what it means to be an exilic people. We have two choices, two different types of people. We can assimilate and disappear into the culture that surrounds us, or we can stand out and make a difference. Which will you do? Who knows, but in standing out you may encourage others also to stand out and be counted for what you believe. Will you, can you do it?

A dangerous people

The church should be full of dangerous people. I don't mean that we are a people of physical violence but we are a people with the capacity for radical change, and radical change can be dangerous. We are encouraged to take the kingdom by force, to have faith which is able to move mountains. We are a people who can pray big prayers to a big God. Christians can change the social landscape through prayer and action. Our history is one of fighting for justice, working against slavery and oppression. In our worship we must be encouraging people to think big and act positively. In the power of God we can bring about radical change into the lives of other, for the benefit of the wider community. Just because society shows disdain for our beliefs, that doesn't mean that we are powerless.

It is because of alternative views of life and the priorities of life that we become dangerous. Our hope is an eternal hope which allows for the possibility for critique and change within the world, a hope that does not disappoint (Rom. 5:5). Only those who have not been assimilated into the societal view can ask the sorts of questions that lead to change. As the church meets together it sings new songs, it dares to dream, it remembers its past and the wonderful things that God has done. In the midst of all of this it believes, and within the fusion a new song emerges: a song of destiny and hope, power and love. It is a song that has the capacity to soar and it is dangerous to hear, because the very hearing of the song may force change to take place.

We must find in our corporate spirit the new song. It will be a song of transformation and possibility. It will be a song that reaffirms our belief in the grace of God and that God is in control. It is a song of sovereignty and hope. It is a dangerous song sung by dangerous people.

In our worship we must encourage people to believe that there is hope; God is in control and we can make a difference.

A playful people
The world is full of certainty. Boundaries on correctness hem us in with images of what is acceptable. There is a subtlety within this. We appear to have more choice today than we have ever had; we seem to have more control. Yet to use the language of jazz, society speaks to us in narrow tones. These boundaries are set and it is clear that to question them pushes us beyond the limits of acceptability. Essentially, there are many tones but only one tune. To quote from Brueggemann:

> Among exiles, it is not necessary or even preferable to engage in monolithic language, that is, language that is one-dimensional, excessively flat, too sure, too serious with much too closure. Monolithic language that smacks of closure is too much an echo of the rhetoric of the empire, precisely what is to be got away from. Whereas the empire needs certitude, exiles need space, room from manoeuvre, breathing opportunities that allow for negotiation, adjudication, ambiguity and playfulness.[48]

While visiting many churches you are faced with a constant rhythm of movement. People from the front direct and control, there is order. Then when the word is preached there is a clear definitive view and the right application. There appears to be little time to gaze upon the beauty of the Lord. Space is not made for people to process and reflect. There is no openness or dialogue. When we think and talk about the glory of God we must also allow people space to think about what that means for them. How does knowing about the glory of God help them in their relationship with their children or in the work place?

Do we have the courage to ask open questions? Can we inspire enough to fire the imagination and allow the worshipping community to dream dreams and bask in their relationship with God, in all its complexity and wonder? If not, why not?

The roadies of God

Over the years I have been to a lot of concerts and conferences and have taken a real interest in seeing the road crew at work. They pay meticulous attention to putting up the structure, making sure that the scaffolding is in place, moving things, working hard to see that the stage is exactly as the band would have it. Then at the end of the show they take it all down, pack away and head on to the next show.

In worship we sometimes take a lot of time putting together a structure. In some churches we call it an 'Order of Service' or a Liturgy; in others it is just what we do. However, sometimes the structure that we have built has become a place of safety and control. The parts of the scaffolding used are those of authority, power, safety and certainty. We know exactly what is expected and what should take place. We have our expectations of when people will stand and sit, sing or speak in tongues, dance and pray. We are inviting people into the Sunday package that has become comfortable to us.

But maybe God is calling some of us to dismantle the staging we have used for a long time. It will not be easy; some of it may have rusted tightly together. All of us will be frightened in case we collapse without the supports. We feel vulnerable, unsure about what may happen next.

But does it force us to pray more and trust in the God who is at the heart of our worship?

I am not calling for chaos or some type of spiritual anarchy, but simply saying that the scaffolding may need to change shape. Maybe the material used in the staging has to be more pliable, less resistant to change so that the unexpected can be embraced. Could it be that part of our role is to continually dismantle and then create new models as appropriate to what God is calling the whole community to do? To be a roadie would be hard work, sometimes dangerous, but think of the satisfaction when it all comes together.

Short interval
- Are there pieces of your worship structure that would no longer get a spiritual safety certificate? They need dismantling, but how will you do it? And what would take their place?

Improvise

I have tried to give a flavour of some of the start up notes for the tunes that I have about worship in this generation and culture. More than anything else I feel that it must centre upon the glory of God. Everything else flows from getting God at the focus of our worship. However, we must find ways for the Christian community to process what they discover of God in such a way that it enables them to live authentic, whole lives within the wider community. To know that God is glorious is a wonderful thing – to know how that relates to being the only Christian in the staff room, or the Christian facing mounting criticism from a non-Christian partner – that is the key to allowing the Christian to stand firm within the culture we are called to live. It is an urgent task which demands creativity, risk and faith. We need to discover truthful, faithful and relevant ways of playing the song that will be authentic to us. It is how we live out the song that defines who we are and what we are called to.

Discipleship

Listening for your name

In his classic book *Discipleship*, David Watson reminds us that the idea of becoming a disciple was not exclusive to the followers of Jesus.[49] Nor was it new to the culture in which Jesus lived and ministered. The verb and noun for disciple appears nearly 300 times in the New Testament. It has several meanings: it can mean a pupil or apprentice or follower. It could also indicate selecting a school of a particular rabbi and seeking to join, live and learn within that structure.

When many of us talk about our own discipleship, we sometimes give the impression that this is what has happened to us; we chose to follow Jesus, the initiative came solely from us. It's as if we look at the various catalogues of possibilities for spiritual life, view the glossy covers, examine the contents page, and conclude that out of all of them, Jesus' offer suits us best. He would be worth following. We can give the impression that we choose Jesus and look forward to all the benefits that come from deciding to pick the Jesus way. But this is not what He said (Mt. 16:24-25).

Sometimes, we present the gospel in a way that gives the impression that everything revolves around us, and Jesus is just there to meet our needs. Are you in need of anything? Then come to Jesus. Do you want happiness in life? Then come to Jesus. Do you want eternal security? Then come to Jesus. In doing so we turn Jesus from the suffering servant into our servant.

To think in this way is to totally misunderstand discipleship. The wonder of discipleship is not in choosing a pattern of teaching or a school of students. Nor is it in picking a person to meet your needs. The wonderful truth is that the initiative lies with Jesus. It is Jesus who called you, not the other way around. Of all the people in the world Jesus called you by name and invited you to follow him. Imagine the wonder of that, the King of the Kings, the Lord of Lords has chosen you. Discipleship begins with an encounter with Jesus that leads to Jesus calling you personally to follow him.

Take my hand

Alison sits in the back of the car as they head down the main street. Her father, who is driving, looks in the mirror at his daughter. He smiles. She has almost grown up – a young lady. She was wearing her new blue dress that matched the colour of her eyes, and her hair was pinned up. To him she was the most beautiful girl in the whole world.

'Are you nervous?' he asked.

She looked up. 'A bit, but I guess it will be OK. I am just worried that no one will want to dance with me. A school dance is really not my scene. At least Karen and Emma will be there so we will have a laugh.'

He looked at her again.

'You are the most special girl in the world. Every guy in the hall will want to dance with you.'

As the car turned into the school car park, Alison noticed that her friends were waiting outside the main doors. Her dad turned around in his seat.

'I'll be back at eleven, have a great time.' He smiled encouragingly as she opened the door and headed away into the crowd making their way to the dance. As she reached her friends, she turned and gave a quick wave before going up the stairs and into the building.

They heard the music as they entered through the doors. The hall was decked out with banners and balloons. The stage was set up for the school band. They were playing some Glenn Miller stuff. A lot of pupils were moving around but there was nobody on the dance floor. As Alison scanned the room she saw that there were a lot of girls standing around on one side and most of the boys on the other side, talking to each other in groups. They found a space and started to shout to each other above the din of the noise. Karen said something funny about one of the boys and they all laughed.

The night was good fun but most of the boys seemed more interested in talking amongst themselves than dancing. The girls laughed and giggled their way through the night. They talked about a whole lot of things: music, school and boys. They talked about Steve. Steve was the guy everyone swooned over. He was in the year above Alison and everybody thought that he was a great guy. He was fashionable, kind and smart. Alison gazed across the room; she knew that Steve was well out of her league. He wouldn't even know who she was.

As the evening drew to a close the band started to play some slow tunes, trying to entice people up onto the dance floor. One or two brave couples were making an attempt. They must be daft thought Alison. As she gazed across the room she noticed that Steve was making his way towards them.

Karen gave Alison a nudge. 'He's suddenly noticed where the good-looking girls are.'

Alison laughed. He got closer and at last stopped in front of her. Alison studied her shoes, not wanting to look up, but she was aware that Steve was looking at her.

'Alison,' he spoke out clearly but quietly, 'will you dance with me?'

She was shocked that he knew her name. Why did he want to dance with her when he could pick anybody in the room? She looked up at him and was aware that she was starting to blush.

'I'm really not any good at dancing,' she said.

'Don't worry, I am' he replied, 'just follow my lead.' With that he put his hand out to her. Nervously, she took it and stepped with him into the unknown of the dance floor.

I like the image of dance as a model for discipleship. Several people have used it and I find it very helpful. Ken Gire in his book *The Divine Embrace* writes, 'There are places he wants to take us on the dance floor, things he wants to show us, feelings he wants to share with us, words he wants to whisper in our ear.'[50]

Suddenly, on receiving the call and following the lead of Jesus, life becomes revealing. New things become clearer as we follow his steps. The relationship that we are invited into is one which grows closer and more intimate, and it changes us forever. In a real sense it is the beginning of life, a moment when one form of existence ends and life in all its fullness begins.

Changing the picture, it is as if you are suddenly able to hear the master musician for the first time, and not only that, but invited to harmonise with him too. As he leads there is improvisation that you never dreamed were possible. It is the denial of the training of the past to enter into the wonder of the new relationship with

Christ. It is to leave the apparent safety of the side of the dance floor, the tax booth, or the fishing boat and in joyous obedience enter into the new relationship which alters existence for ever.

Going back to the story of Alison for a moment, the main point that I want to make from this story is that Alison would never have gone onto the dance floor on her own account. It was only because someone saw her, went over to her and called her to go with him. It was first an initiative, then an encounter and finally a call to trust. So it is with the beginning of discipleship. It starts with the initiative of God in Jesus Christ. If Jesus did not know your name and call you then there would be no opportunity to follow. This is so important because it is about the desire of a loving God to call you into a relationship with him. Of all the things in the universe, God wants to have a relationship with you. He knows your name and he decided to draw near to you and call you to follow. This was not because of anything about you. In the world's eyes you may not be that gifted or special. You may not have the charisma that will get you noticed in the world, but in pure loving grace God has called to you. He has invited you to leave behind the old to follow him wherever that might lead. Will you follow?

I know you

Think about these words from the beginning of Psalm 139:

> O LORD, you have examined my heart
>   and know everything about me.
> You know when I sit down or stand up.
> You know my every thought from far away.

You chart the path ahead of me
    and tell me where to stop and rest.
Every moment you know where I am.
You know what I am going to say
    even before I say it LORD.
You both precede and follow me.
You place your hand of blessing on my head.
Such knowledge is too wonderful for me,
    too great for me to know! (Ps. 139:1-6)

I believe that this wonderful care and knowledge is central to our calling as disciples, and it is seen in the calling of the first disciples in John 1. I imagine it like this. It was the day after John the Baptist gave witness to who Jesus was (Jn. 1:29,35). John was in the same area and was chatting to a couple of his disciples. As they were deep in conversation Jesus passed close by them. John's attention is drawn again to the character of Jesus, and he makes the same comment that he had used the previous day. 'Look, the Lamb of God' he says (v. 35). The disciples may have thought that this was a reference to the prophet Jeremiah who wrote about 'a gentle lamb' (Jer. 11:19), or perhaps the daily sacrifice or scapegoat bearing people's sins. Whatever they thought, the disciples hear John use this title again, get up and head towards Jesus (v. 37).

When they get close enough Jesus turns and confronts them. Looking straight at them he directs a question at them, a question that has so many layers of meaning.

'What do you want?'

They look at each other and wonder how to reply. 'Rabbi, where are you staying?'

In fact they have not answered Jesus' question at all. Yet they were giving an indication that what they wanted was to spend time with him.

In kindness Jesus does not press them but gives them a great opportunity. His gaze is one of warmth and invitation: 'Come and you will see,' he replies.

The disciples are thrilled; they had hoped to spend some time with Jesus but he was under no obligation to spend any time dealing with questions they might have. Theirs had been a tentative question but Jesus had responded with a huge opportunity.

They travel along the road together and then spent most of the day with Jesus. We don't know what they talked about or what questions Jesus answered for them. Perhaps they wanted to know about John's title for Jesus. They must have talked about who Jesus was. Whatever the heart of the conversation, it is clear that it had a huge impact upon at least one of John's disciples, Andrew. He heads straight for his brother Simon (v. 41). Andrew is so excited that he tracks down his brother, who was maybe fixing fishing nets or repairing the boat.

As Andrew approaches, he looks up. What was wrong, why was Andrew in such a great rush? Had something happened to the family? Could there have been an accident? Andrew grasps Simon by the shoulders and looks into his eyes. He takes a few deep breaths, getting his breath back. 'We have found the Messiah.' Simon didn't know what to say; he had never seen his brother like this before. 'You *have* to come and meet him for yourself.' With that, Andrew gripped Simon by the hand and led him on the journey that would bring him to Jesus.

Simon was never a shy man and when they got to the place where Jesus was staying he stepped forward. Jesus looked up from where he had been staying and spoke to Simon, '"You are Simon son of John. You will be called Cephas" (which when translated is Peter)' (Jn. 1:42).

The next day Jesus surprised people by saying that he was heading for Galilee. As Jesus headed towards his destination he encountered Philip. We don't know whether Philip knew Andrew and Simon Peter, but we are told that he came from the same town as these two new disciples. Jesus made contact with Philip and after that encounter Jesus tells Philip to follow him.

Soon after Philip had met and heard the call of Jesus he decides he must tell his friend Nathanael. Like Andrew before him, Philip is really excited after meeting Jesus, and as soon as he meets Nathanael he has got to tell him about the great discovery that he has made (Jn. 1:45-49).

'Listen Nathanael, I have great news for you. We have found him.'

'Found who?' replies Nathanael. Philip can hardly contain his excitement. 'The one Moses spoke about in the Law and about whom the prophets also wrote.'

Nathanael is captivated by Philip's enthusiasm. 'Who is it that you are talking about Philip?'

'It is Jesus of Nazareth; He is the son of Joseph.'

An unbelieving look spread across his face. 'You can't be serious. Surely not Nazareth! Can anything good come from there?' Philip had expected this scornful response; but he also knew that all he had to do was get Nathanael to Jesus.

'Come and see.'

They travelled together and eventually came to Jesus. He looked at them both but his attention settled upon Nathanael. Jesus gazed up at Nathanael and said in a clear voice, 'Truly here is an Israelite who is an honest man.' Those around turned to gaze at the new arrival that had caused such a reaction. Nathanael was surprised by the words of Jesus. Unsure of what to say, Nathanael can only ask how Jesus could know him. Jesus responded by answering, 'I saw you while you were still under the fig tree, before Philip called you.'

How could Jesus possibly have known where Nathanael had been before Philip had searched him out? The words of Jesus certainly had a real impact upon this honest man: 'Rabbi, you are the Son of God; you are the King of Israel.' By these words Nathanael was acknowledging Jesus as the Messiah. He was the promised one, the fulfilment just as Philip had said.

John's account of the call of the first disciples is marvellous and highlights several things that are really important for us to grasp as we live out the call of Jesus on our own lives.

Nothing escapes his notice

It is both encouraging and challenging to know that God knows everything about us. Jesus could sum up Nathanael's character in a few words. He could tell Nathanael what he had been doing and where he had been. What an amazing thing to learn, that Jesus knew his character better than he knew it himself.

When Jesus called you to follow, he already knew everything about you. He knew your strengths and weaknesses. He saw the huge disasters that you had got into and the things that you are really embarrassed about. You may have thought that there were things you could hide away, things that nobody would ever know. Jesus has always known everything about you.

As I thought about this two images came into my mind. I am driving from Perth down to Edinburgh. It's early in the morning and there are not many cars on the road. The sun is rising and it's going to be a beautiful spring day. I reach down to the CDs and put on the American singer/songwriter Steven Curtis Chapman. I like his 'Declaration' album. I crank up the volume and as it starts I break into song. I sing loudly and mostly off-key, but I don't care. I don't care because nobody else can hear me. Then I think about the fact that Jesus is actually seeing and hearing this. I hope that he has the capacity either to become tone deaf or can make my toneless bawling into something acceptable. I think my heart is in the right place; it's my vocal chords that are the real problem.

The second image is one from the first *Harry Potter* movie. Early on there is a particularly Dickensian incident. The camera fixes upon the face of Harry as he is slowly starting to awake. His aunt bangs upon his bedroom door yelling for him to get up and help with the breakfast. It then becomes clear that he is forced to sleep in the cupboard under the stairs. He is locked away from view, contained in a tiny space with only a few possessions – discarded and uncared for. Then, as if to emphasize the difficulty of Harry's situation, Dudley, Harry's cousin comes down the stairs and takes particular delight in jumping on the stairs, knowing that dust and dirt will fall upon Harry.

I've always thought that this is a particularly poignant scene. The family don't know how to handle Harry; they keep him down and try to repress him. At night he is locked away, out of sight and out of mind.

I think that we do the same with incidents in our lives. There are hurts, doubts and sins that we lock away in some recess in our hearts and minds, hoping that we can hide them both from our own view and others. By doing this we can present ourselves in the way that we think would be acceptable. We only allow others to glimpse the parts of our lives that we are comfortable with, the rest we shove in some cupboard. There are times in my life when it would have had to have been a pretty big hiding space. This is what is so amazing about the glorious grace of God found in Jesus. Jesus sees past the cupboard door.

He sees everything there, and yet still he chooses to draw near to me and to you. Like Nathanael, the fact that Jesus knows us and still desires to engage with us should humble us and lead to serious reflection upon the character of Jesus. It should lead us into an attitude of praise.

Short interval

- Read Psalm 121. Can you turn this psalm into your personal psalm of praise? Or you could write your own psalm of praise to God.

- Call upon God; praise him for who he is and what he has done. Let our hearts be filled with praise and thanks and awe!

He takes the initiative

It was the first conference of its type that I had been invited to. I knew a few of the people who would be there, but as I drove towards the venue uncertainty gripped me. I wasn't sure that I would feel all that comfortable. My mind flies in lots of directions: I think a lot in story and image and prefer dialogue to lecture. Although the topics sounded interesting and the list of speakers was impressive I was nervous.

I turned right, through the gates of the hotel, and headed up the long drive. Pulling into the car park there were many people getting out of cars obviously heading for the conference – mostly men well turned out in shirt and tie. I scanned those making their way in through the large glass doors of the hotel, looking for someone to latch onto, but I didn't recognize anyone.

In the foyer I picked up a coffee and looked around at those huddled in groups. I said 'Hi' to one or two people and smiled at others. Then I walked into the large hall. At both ends there were bookstalls and information areas. I wandered over to look at what was on display, looking at the books for sale and checking my watch to see how long it would be before things got under way. The words of the Sting song about being an alien in New York[51] ran through my mind. Placing a book back on the stand I smiled at the woman behind the desk and went to find a seat.

I had just sat down when I saw a face that I recognized. He was an older church leader, a man of God who had been greatly used throughout his ministry. I had been introduced to him on two occasions; at both times I had been part of a larger group of people chatting to him. I watched him for a while. He put his Bible on a chair and then sat down; several friends came and joined him. Minutes before the meeting was about to start I felt a tap on my shoulder. I turned. It was him. He was smiling down at me. I stood up and shook the hand on offer.

'Fred' he said, 'how are you? I have been hearing good things about what God is doing in Perth. Are you encouraged?' He spoke with a genuine interest and earnestness. We chatted for a few minutes as the meeting was getting underway.

As I think back to that small and apparently insignificant event I wonder why it has stayed with me for all these years. I am sure that it is because it told me something about the man and something about myself. It showed graciousness on his part: he took the initiative to come to talk to me even though we had hardly met. Not only that, but he had remembered my name. Here was a man who was interested in people. On my part I remember feeling greatly encouraged by his interest and the fact that he had remembered who I was.

Naming is vitally important. Our names say a lot about us. They say something of our family and our culture.

They show that we have some worth or status or value in the consciousness of someone else. Someone at some time in the past thought we were significant enough to be given a name. For someone to remember our name is for them to acknowledge that we have made some impression upon them, or that they have a particular care or interest in us. For relationships to develop we must get beyond seeing others as nameless. We look forward to sharing and developing a relationship with someone we have come to know. Part of that knowing has been learning and remembering their name.

Names are very important in the Bible and in the unfolding of God's work of salvation too – from the names God gave, to the ones he changed. Think of Jacob in Genesis 32:22-32 as he wrestles with a man until daybreak. Jacob has a tough time but he doesn't give up. The man sees that he cannot overcome Jacob and so he touches Jacob's hip and the hip is wrenched out of the socket. Still Jacob keeps going. When daybreak arrives the man that Jacob is fighting wants to go but Jacob will not stop until he receives a blessing. The blessing comes in the form of a new name. The man tells Jacob: 'Your name will no longer be Jacob, but Israel, because you have struggled with God and with men and have overcome' (v. 28). Jacob's change of character and status is seen in a renaming.

Talking about this incident Derek Kidner comments, 'After the maiming, combativeness had turned into dogged dependence, and Jacob emerged broken, named and blest. His limping would be a lasting proof of the reality of the struggle; it had been no dream and there was sharp judgement to it. The new name would attest his new standing.'[52] God knew who Jacob was, and what he was to become.

There are reminders here of the account between Jesus and Simon in John 1. Jesus begins the conversation by

calling Simon by name but then tells him that he will be
known by another name: 'You will be called Cephas
(which, when translated, is Peter)' (v. 42). This name,
which means rock, shows that Jesus not only knew who
he was but also what he would become in Jesus.

What a wonderful thought! Not only does Jesus know
us by name, he knows what we can become. He has plans
that only he knows about, plans to change and transform
us.

Think back to the encouragement that I felt from the
church leader remembering who I was. How much
greater is it that Jesus cares enough to call us by name. We
are not unknown, unrecognizable or forgotten by him:
He knows our name!

Spend time with me

In the story of the calling of the first disciples as found in
John 1 we have already noted some wonderful things
about Jesus. Nothing escaped his notice and yet knowing
what he knew he still entered into dialogue with
Nathanael. Not only that, but he began his conversation
with Simon Peter by addressing him by his name and
then changing that name. Think of how Simon must have
felt; he was not nameless to Jesus. Jesus knew who Simon
was and what he could become.

Perhaps the most amazing thing of all is that Jesus
allowed these people – the seeker, the prejudice, those
who came and those who were brought – to encounter
him. Jesus gave them the most precious thing of all. He
gave them time. Jesus allowed people the opportunity to
encounter him and to glimpse the possibilities of
fellowship with him. It was time given so that the curtain
may be pulled back from a mundane existence, opening
up the endless possibilities of life as God intended it.

We talk about the need for quality time: quality time with our families and for ourselves, and I believe that is really important. Everyone who encountered Jesus got quality time, his full attention. To focus so much energy on people as individuals must have been hugely draining and called for great openness and vulnerability. Yet it was the Jesus way. How different that is to the way in which our society lives. Two separate things highlighted this for me recently.

It was late in the evening and everyone had gone to bed. There is a room in our house that I find really peaceful (not a word usually used in connection with our house!). It has a wooden floor and the walls are painted in soothing colours with various prints hanging on them. There is a sofa and a few lounge chairs scattered around but no TV or CD player and so it is used rarely by the rest of the family. So with a few magazines under my arm and a cup of Chai tea in the other, I headed into my favourite sanctuary.

The magazine that grabbed my attention had a front cover that boldly stated, 'Special Issue 100: The A-list of the world's most influential people.'[53] The list was extensive, from Condoleezza Rice to Bono and Vladamir Putin to Oprah Winfrey. I searched through the list and picked out those that I had either never heard of or was particularly interested in. I gobbled up the information about Jerry Bruckheimer having a golden touch with mass media, and the success of Michael Dell in developing a computer company. In the main these were driven people, people with great energy, vision and insight.

In the midst of all this greatness I began to wonder whether any of these folk would have the time to stop and allow others to encounter them. I wondered if being vulnerable and open would have been high on the list of important characteristics. Would any allow strangers to follow, question and bring others to them? I did not feel critical towards anybody on the list, rather I marvelled all the more at Jesus. As I sat sipping my tea I thought of the most important person who ever lived. The one with the most drive and vision and intellect and I pictured him stopping, smiling and saying 'Come and see for yourselves.'

The meeting started at 10:30, coffee at 10. It was a planning meeting for church leaders. We milled around chatting to one another and then at 10:30 we moved through to another room and the meeting began with prayer. After the prayer handouts were distributed I looked around the table and was suddenly struck by the fact that we nearly all had large time manager diaries, like a row of big slabs they lay on the table.

'Before we come to the business of the day we will have a reading from Scripture,' the chair of the meeting said.

Suddenly, hands shot to inside jacket pockets, like cowboys at a shoot-out as pocket New Testaments were pulled out. What caught my attention was the contrast between the huge diaries and tiny Bibles. Against the grandeur of the office organizers signalling just how busy people were, these Bibles were small and hidden, pulled out in acceptable company. I think that God was speaking to me. Where did our priorities really lie?

Jesus was the ultimate time manager. He led and directed; his was the true life of purpose. He set himself towards Jerusalem and was governed by the will of God. Yet his heart was for the individual and he made himself available to others so that through an encounter with him their lives may be changed.

What a wonderful thing to consider that Jesus allows you to encounter him and gives you the time that you need you to discover who he is. Like the early disciples you may have heard something about Jesus that drew you in and challenged you. You may have known people who were Christians and seen how different they were. Whatever it was, something pulled you like a magnet until you encountered Jesus.

The amazing thing is that Jesus was willing and gracious enough to allow you to meet him. In contrast to the March hare from *Alice in Wonderland*, who, watch in hand is half listening and half thinking about something else, Jesus regards you as too important for that. It is out of this encounter with Jesus that the call comes from Jesus, the call of discipleship. The call to 'come and follow me' (see Lk. 18:18-30).

Come follow me

The call from Jesus to come and follow is found in all four gospels. It is directed towards fishermen and tax-collectors, rich and poor. The good news is for all. Let me introduce you to two people who knew a lot about money: Matthew the tax-collector and the rich young man. Worlds apart, yet both had contact with the Son of God. In Luke chapter 18 we are given an account of the conversation between Jesus and this rich young man. The young man is full of confidence and approaches Jesus with a question.

'Good teacher, what must I do to inherit eternal life?'

Obviously, there is no beating about the bush with this guy. No 'how are you?' or 'do you mind if I ask you a question?' A direct enquiry: he certainly doesn't lack self-confidence. Perhaps that is his real problem.

Jesus reminds him that only God is good and then points the young man to the Ten Commandments.

The confidence of the man comes to the fore again in his reply. 'All these I have kept since I was a boy.'

There is a real sense of self-righteousness in this reply. This man has a disturbing confidence in his own ability and morality. As Darrell L. Bock comments, '. . . now the man's problem begins to surface. He is confident that he can stand before God on his own merits.'[54]

Jesus wastes no time. He tells the young man that he still lacks one thing: 'Sell everything that you have and give it to the poor, and you will have treasure in heaven. Then come, follow me.'

The man came asking about how to gain eternal life and Jesus offered him the possibility of treasure in heaven and a relationship with God. However, to gain these things the young man had to put all distractions behind him; the wealth on which he relied would have to be put to one side. This was too much for the man and he left upset and disappointed. The young man had the encounter with Jesus, heard the call, had the chance for relationship yet went away sad. What a tragic response.

Matthew was working at his tax booth. He would have been collecting or counting money. Jesus saw him sitting there. Jesus immediately called him to come and 'follow me' (Mt. 9:9). Matthew got up and followed. There was the encounter, then the call then the response from this tax-collector. Not only does he get up and leave his work place and join the other disciples, he also wants to introduce his friends to Jesus. Matthew was happy to be marked out as someone who followed Jesus. What about you? Is there anything that is hindering you coming to Jesus, anything that you need to cast aside as you continue in your Christian life?

There are three final things that are important to think about with regard to the call of Jesus on your life. Firstly, the call is a personal one. Jesus does not call you as part of a large group. He calls you personally. As he called Matthew from the tax-booth (Mt. 9:9-13) or Andrew from his life as a fisherman (Jn. 1:35-41) so he calls you to follow him. Knowing all there is to know he has called you. He wants you to hear the call and to follow.

It is also a relational call. We are called not to a set of rules or some clever dogma. We are called to trust in a person. We are called into a personal relationship with Jesus, believing that he who calls us is faithful and true. The theologian Karl Barth sums it up in this way, 'The possible content of this command [follow me] is that this or that specific person to whom it is given should come to, and follow and be with the one who gives it. In this one, and the relationship that it establishes between him and the one he calls, a good deal more is involved. But there is nothing apart from him and this relationship.'[55]

This becomes a question of faith. Do you trust the one who has called? Do you want to hand your life over to this one who comes and calls you by name? Think for a minute about it. This Jesus who has called you to follow is compassionate and loving. He is the one who fed the hungry crowds and stilled the raging storms with a word of command. He is Jesus, the Son of God who looked at a city and wept over its unbelief. The one who calls you is he who loves you as no other can. He was willing to give his life that you might live.

This is the one who calls. He is not some uncaring demigod messing around with life for the fun of it, like some character from the movie *Troy*. He is fully God and fully man who came to save you. Yet not only is he Saviour, he is also Lord. The Greek word translated Lord, (*Kyrios*) can sometimes be a general term of courtesy, like sir, but when it is used of Jesus it means master, or one with power.

'I am he'

Everyone remembers the story of Thomas, which is recounted in the Gospel of John. Thomas hadn't been with the other disciples when the risen Jesus had appeared to them. Perhaps he was so hurt and disillusioned that he needed some space. I guess it would have been a place damp with discouragement and disappointment. Whatever the reason, Thomas misses Jesus' appearance. However, I don't think that he could miss the change of attitude in the disciples. They tell Thomas that they have seen the Lord. Thomas can't take in what they have said, he just can't deal with it. How does he react? Speaking through a fog of disappointment, confusion and doubt he tells them: 'Unless I see the nail marks in his hands and put my finger where the nails were, and put my hand into his side, I will not believe it' (Jn. 20:25b).

About a week later Jesus again appears to the disciples; this time Thomas is there with all the others. I wonder what the last week had been like for him as he watched the other disciples. Jesus turns his attention to Thomas. There is silence in the room as Jesus commands Thomas, 'Put your fingers here; see my hands. Reach out take your hand and put it into my side. Stop doubting and believe.'

In the face of this loving challenge how does Thomas reply? 'My Lord and my God.' By using the term Lord, Thomas is saying 'You are Master, King. Everything revolves around you. Jesus, you are the one with all authority. My life belongs to you.' The implication is that Jesus deserves whole-life obedience. That to follow is to leave everything else behind and life in a different way.

Whole-life commitment

What does it mean to follow? This may seem a strange question, yet I feel that it is a vital one, particularly in our generation. As we have already noted, ours is a generation that has difficulties with long-term commitment. In many aspects of our lives we have moved to a place where we are comfortable walking away, letting go or moving on if things are no longer relevant or helpful to us. We live in a place of pragmatic relativism. In the practical things of our lives there are few absolutes. Things that were felt to be important yesterday have no significance today, society moves quickly from one thing to another. Whether it is work, relationships or beliefs, we are comfortable with moving on to the new and leaving the old behind.

However, to follow Jesus is to give a whole-life response to him. It is to live within a new matrix where obedience to the call of Jesus is the most important and enduring mark of our lives. It is to learn from the master and to keep learning for the whole of life. This is not always easy – it was never intended to be – but without the desire to obey there can be no discipleship. To be the best that we can be for Christ is to submit the life that we have been given over to the will and purpose that God has for it. It is to abandon the old life, with the priorities and to see following Jesus as everything.

Thinking about jazz as an illustration, it would be fair to say that many talented musicians never reached their potential because they did not give their all to the practice and study that was required. The desire to put the music first was not strong enough. Sometimes it's easy to get caught up in distractions and lose sight of what is important.

For the disciple what is required is the passion to follow Jesus at all costs. To be a person who desires to

obey Jesus so that he might be glorified in the life of the
disciple. This is not an easy task, nor is it one that can be
undertaken lightly. It is whole-life commitment and it
will be costly. I think that it is vital in today's cultural
environment that we do as Jesus did and stress the cost of
discipleship. If obedience and cost are key features of
what it is to follow Jesus then we do both individuals and
the church a great disservice by not encouraging people
to count the cost before starting the journey. People need
to understand that life will never be the same if they
accept the call onto the spiritual dance floor.

Think it through

When teaching about commitment Jesus made it clear
that it was better not to start than to begin and give up.
Some of Jesus teaching on commitment is astonishing.
Think about these verses

> 'If you want to be my follower you must love me
> more than your own father and mother, wife and
> children, brothers and sisters – yes, more than your
> own life. Otherwise, you cannot be my disciple. And
> you cannot be my disciple if you do not carry your
> own cross and follow me. But don't begin until you
> count the cost' (Lk. 14:26-28, NLT).

Jesus then gives illustrations about cost from the realms
of construction and warfare to underline the point in
the verses following. While there may be several interpretations of these verses three things do appear to be very
clear.

- It is impossible to be a disciple if you do not love Jesus above everything else.
- It is impossible to be a disciple if you are not willing to enter fully into the new life including the suffering and sorrow that will be involved.

- You cannot be a disciple if you have not counted the cost before you start.

What we are being called to do is to live in relationship with our Lord and in following him we are called to give up any other ambitions than to follow him. All other relationships are insignificant compared to the relationship that we have with Jesus. Part of the badge of honour of following Jesus is to carry a cross. We are only able to carry our cross because he carried his. The cross for us, while difficult to carry, is also part of the privilege of knowing Jesus. To carry the cross is to be no longer controlled by an old way of living but to enter into the Jesus way; it shows the desire to know him, no matter the cost.

Dietrich Bonhoeffer, commenting on the cross in the life of the believer, says 'the cross is not the terrible end to an otherwise God-fearing and happy life, but it meets us at the beginning of our communion with Christ. When Christ calls a man, he bids him to come and die.'[56]

This is the great paradox for us, that in order for us to truly live as disciples we must first be ready to die to everything else. This dying to the old life and its complex series of ambitions, hopes and relationships enables us to live in all fullness through our relationship with Jesus Christ. He is the one who loved us and gave himself for us and calls us into union with himself.

The call to follow Jesus is a radical call, involving a lifetime of service and obedience as well as love and fellowship. To come and follow Jesus is to turn fully in a new direction. This is something that needs thinking through and weighing up.

In the past when I have given marriage preparation classes I would spend some time on the words from the Book of Common Order concerning our attitude to marriage: Marriage 'should not be undertaken carelessly, lightly or selfishly but reverently, responsibly and after serious thought.'[57] This could be applied to the way in which we should consider discipleship. To heed the call of Jesus as Lord should not be done lightly because it is to enter into a life of both love and obedience.

Caught in a two-fold folly

I have tried to highlight two major aspects of our life as a disciple of Jesus. The first is that it is important that we never lose sight of the wonder of our calling in Christ. To be invited into a loving relationship with Jesus is the greatest thing that could ever happen to us. It is a wonderful act of grace that the King of Kings might want us to be his followers. There is joy on the journey because of who it is that has called us and where he might lead us.

However, it is also correct to stress that the life of the disciple is a life given over to following Jesus. It does not mean that we will be perfect, but it does mean that we have died to the old life and now live for Jesus. This new life of following requires obedience and will lead to conflict and suffering. To follow Jesus is to take up our own cross.

I have stressed these two areas because I believe that we have, as a church, failed to address both these parts of the calling and so led people into an unbalanced view of discipleship. We focus on one to the neglect of the other.

The result? We are in danger of advocating two extreme forms of discipleship: legalistic discipleship that centres around rules and regulations rather than relationship; and low-maintenance, low-cost discipleship that integrates rather than separates from the culture around. Let us look briefly at these twin traps.

It's what you do and the way you do it!

When someone hears the call of God on their lives and turns from their old life to the new they are often overloaded with information. Information about what is expected of them. Quickly we learn that to be a disciple is to follow certain regulations. Stress is placed upon how much we read the Bible, what services we should attend, how we should pray and the importance of attending prayer meetings. We sometimes go as far as to suggest what Bible translation people use and how they spend their money. While there is nothing wrong with any of these things the problem is the attitude that underlies them.

If I could put it this way, before people come to respond to the call of Jesus we spend most of our time telling them about him. Once people have responded to Jesus we spend most of our time talking about the church, and particularly the lifestyle that is acceptable to the church. Rather than reminding people that discipleship is following Jesus, and therefore having a deepening relationship with him, we stress the outward signs that are expected of those who follow. Discipleship then becomes more about appearance than inward reality and rules rather than relationship. It is easy to rob someone of the wonder of a love relationship and replace it with a burden that takes a form of legalism. I think that the temptation to place modernist church expectations on new disciples has led to many feeling weighed down

under the yoke of demands that come from the church.[58]
Subtly the language of grace, forgiveness, hope and
mystery seems to be replaced by the tones of duty,
expectation and consistency. We are encouraged not so
much to delight in the journey but to be constantly aware
of the dangers of falling away.

Reflecting upon his early Christian life and the
constant fear of falling away, Eugene Peterson notes that
it was only later, when he realized that 'living as a
Christian is not walking a tightrope without a safety net,
high above breathless crowd, many of whom would like
nothing better than the morbid thrill of seeing you fall, it
is sitting secure in the fortress.'[59] We are secure because of
the gracious and wonderful call of the Saviour. While all
the disciplines of the Christian life are important we must
make sure that we are stressing their importance in
connection with following Jesus. It is not about doing
these things for their own sake. It is doing them because
through them God may speak by the Spirit in ways that
enable you to follow. It is my conviction that many of us,
when dealing with new disciples, have not stressed
clearly enough that the disciplines of the church are there
so that God – who is continually at work – will work in
our lives in amazing ways which draw us closer to the
one who loves us with an everlasting love.

Low-cost DIY Christianity

If we have been guilty as a church of turning discipleship
into legalism then the other great danger is to minimize
the cost involved in following Jesus. In a world where
commitment is a relative term the temptation for the
church is to offer a low-maintenance, low-cost salvation.
To seek to appeal to the wider community we can try to
give that community a faith that will be palatable to it. To

do that we simply remove from our discussions anything that might put people off following Jesus. We provide a package that fits the culture well, but is it any longer discipleship as Jesus intended? In a culture where people have the right to make all their own choices and want control over their own lives the temptation for the church is to no longer stress obedience and lordship.

Sometimes in our desire to be understood by the cultures that we are trying to engage with we can find ourselves losing the very distinctive that makes us counter-cultural. In finding ways of communicating the message of Jesus into an individualistic and capitalist culture we are not only altering our language so that we can be understood, but often unintentionally altering the message. We want to find the language to make the gospel known, but if we are not careful it is the message itself that we are changing. It is hard work to find ways of communicating ideas like sacrifice, obedience, death to the old life, and so on.

It's not always easy to live in and communicate with a culture and yet remain counter-cultural, but that is the challenge to the church. We are called to be different and trust that the radical nature of that distinctive call will have an impact upon the wider community. We must find and use ways of making the message known but we must not change the radical dynamic of the message simply to gain the approval of any culture. I believe that as we encounter the ever hastening death of Christendom and engage with more generations of people who are totally new to the gospel our desire to be understood may lead us to simply ignore the parts of the message that we find hardest to explain. At the heart of the message is Jesus Christ as Saviour and Lord. It is about his death, resurrection and call to a radical new life in him, where we die to the old and embrace the new.

Consider again Jesus' encounter with the rich young ruler in Luke 18:18-25. It occurs to me that he would be the ideal candidate for many of our churches. He is young, which will help bring down the average age of the congregation; he is wealthy, which will help the church finances. He has influence, which will give us a voice, and he is spiritually open. Here is a guy who is seeking, questioning. Not only would he make a good member but he's surely a potential leader, perhaps running young people's events. Just as he is becoming interested would we really challenge him about his wealth? Would we love the young man enough to put our own self-interest aside and explain the need to put Jesus first and what the consequences of that might be for him?

Short interval

• Is your church working hard enough to be understood by those in the wider community? In what ways could it develop that work?

• As your church has tried to disciple people are there signs of more connection to church but less to Jesus? If so how might you correct the imbalance? Never lose the wonder of God's call on your life.

Community living

We have considered the call and cost of discipleship, but what about the community? Have you ever thought that much of Jesus' work with the original followers took place as a group? They travelled the road together. They saw the miracles and reflected upon the parables. They ate together and questioned together. The disciples shared in a group dynamic with Jesus at the centre. Even when they were sent out to put into practice what they had been taught they did so together. While the call to follow had been personal their ongoing discipleship was a shared experience.

Discipleship is a community activity. In the individualistic world in which we live the community aspect to our growth as disciples can be forgotten. The New Testament is very clear that the Christians grew as a distinct people. Their corporate allegiance to Jesus Christ enabled them to follow in the way that Jesus had called them to. They were one people with Jesus at the centre. He was their Lord who continued his ministry in and through them.

Think too of the early church. We have already considered their commitment as believers and how this was acted out in communal living, a community. They were living out the theology of being one body. Their connectedness was seen in their giving, praying and in their devotion to the name of Jesus and to the Lord's Supper. Their equipping for following was done as a body and the foundations for the journey were played out together. The point that I am making is that we cannot see discipleship in isolation from our life as part of the Christian community. Therefore we must find ways within our communities for growing as disciples together. It is in the body that we gain strength and encouragement as we see ourselves connected to the rest of the family of believers. While the responsibility to follow is ours, the signposts of where to go and the love that enables us to follow also comes from our sense of belonging. It is together that we chart the course.

An example of this for me is found in the writing of John Swinton. In *Resurrecting the Person* he challenges the church with regard to its friendship and care for those with mental health issues. I found it a challenging read

because it affects me as a disciple and as part of the body
of Christ. The idea of friendship with those who may
reject that love effects my call to follow Jesus. At the same
time it is something that needs to be shared and worked
out within the body of believers. John writes

> Because of the nature of the illness, there is always
> the possibility that the offer of friendship will be
> rejected. Church communities who are willing to
> offer such friendships must be prepared for disap-
> pointment, hurt and rejection. The flip side of love
> and genuine caring is anxiety, pain and suffering
> and the possibility of rejection. The concept of
> friendship based on the friendships of Jesus has
> certain messianic overtones that relate to issues of
> suffering and sacrifice.[60]

These words highlight real issues in my walk with Jesus.
How do I love those who may reject that love? What do I
learn about my relationship with the Lord when I reflect
upon the fact that the other side of true love is anxiety
and pain? How do I meet Jesus in the pain of rejection
and get the strength to go on loving? These are big issues
for me. However, as John points out, they are issues for
the whole Christian community. It is as a community that
we have to pray and share our anxieties. It is as we come
together that we can seek the help of the Holy Spirit to
gain insight and help when we feel overwhelmed and
tempted to give up. It is through the ministry of others
that I can go back into the world and face the possibilities
of the new day, knowing that Jesus will lead me and that
my job is to be faithful: that the one who calls me is able.

Let's do it – let's fall in love

Here it might be helpful to reconsider how we can help people grow as disciples of Jesus. Can we create small groups where we can explore honestly the issues that are involved in the day-to-day call to take up our cross and follow Jesus? This could involve meeting in a coffee house, allowing people to ask questions, learn and laugh together in an environment that is relaxed and open. Through sharing, the discussion may go in all sorts of directions as the group grows together. As the group deepens so will people's level of trust, and they will be able to share things that help them in their difficult journey as disciples of Jesus.

We could compare this to musicians who, getting together to hear each other's tunes, end up jamming together to make new things happen. Imagine Jelly Roll Morton, King Oliver and Louis Armstrong laughing together in a smoky New Orleans bar, helping one another with insight and enthusiasm. In the same way a synchronicity of spiritual life can lead people to overcome long held barriers in their journey of faith.

It really doesn't matter where the group meets, or how it is done: what is important is that the church as a body is providing a means by which it helps each part to grow in love with the one they have been called to follow. It is a big mistake to think that Christians are coping well with the environment that we are living in. We will find the going really tough, and for some they give up on following. While we will never be able to fully prevent that I do believe that disciples are crying out for support – support that is not based around tasks to be done or programmes to be followed – but open, honest loving support from others travelling in the same direction.

Short interval

- Are we so busy doing things that we don't spend enough time talking to other Christians about following Jesus?

- Who could benefit from a phone call or a visit, or a cheerful smile at the next church meeting?

Play your story

Recently, I heard an interesting interview on the radio. The subject was a new initiative taking place within British athletics. The plan was to provide mentors for the best up and coming athletes. The mentors would be Olympic gold medallists and world record holders – those who had reached the highest pinnacle of their chosen sport but had now retired. Meeting regularly with a few of these potentials, their job was to share what was required for the potential to be unlocked. Talent was not enough. What was required was hard work, the right lifestyle choices and the attitude of mind. The mentors had gone down that road and knew what it cost. They knew how it felt to get an injury, or when training has not gone as well as hoped, and so they can become a motivator and encourager. The mentors can explain how they coped with difficult times and still prevailed.

In a sense what these people were doing was simply passing on their tune. The rhythm of their lives was being shared with others: they had travelled the road themselves.

In the church we have lots of people who are following Jesus, and have been for some time. They know that there are some really steep inclines and they have passed through periods of doubt and uncertainty. It does not mean that they have all the answers or that they have arrived, but it does mean that they have stayed on course so far. To use the mentor idea, why don't we use these people's life experiences to help others? How good it would be to link new disciples with those more well-travelled disciples: to help talk through the early stages of the journey of faith. This is particularly important when the new converts come from a non-churched background and have little knowledge of basic Christian teaching.

Why should we be serious about mentoring? There are huge advantages for a church to be *intentional* about mentoring, i.e. to have a plan about how it mentors new believers. I would like to suggest a few. Firstly, it gives an opportunity for a new convert to build a meaningful relationship with a more mature Christian: someone who will pray and share and be available as a guide. Whilst the group setting may be daunting to the new convert, the one-on-one meeting allows them to question and challenge the mentor about pressing spiritual matters.

Secondly, it causes the mentor to reflect upon their own spiritual walk and to consider things anew. The enthusiasm and openness of the new disciple may re-energize the spiritual life of the mentor, and so the relationship can be reciprocal. Thirdly, it gives validity to the mentor's experience of God. It says to that person that we as a church are grateful for your life as a Christian.

Mentoring is far too important to leave to chance, it requires some thought and action so that the right people can be used and supported as they mentor. We are living in a time when old certainties are being questioned and stable meaningful relationships are difficult to maintain. Therefore it is vital that the person who hears the call to follow very quickly finds a relationship within the Christian community which enables them to be nurtured

and supported. It may be that the mentor (the represen-
tative part of the body) is the key link that enables the
new disciple to cope with the challenges to leaving the
world behind. It could be the only thing that the church
can provide that makes any sense.

Picture the new convert who comes from a third
generation of non-churched people, who hears the gospel
and responds to the gracious call of Jesus. For them,
growth may not come in an organized setting. Maybe the
way we do worship will be too complex and ordered to
help. Could it be that discipling will happen through
texting and conversation; that worship will be walking in
the park or sharing a meal together? For some this may
be the way of growth until the place of the whole
community begins to make sense. While providing a
tailor-made programme for everyone is beyond us,
surely spending time finding the right people who can
mentor is a task that we should be implementing now.

When I look back to my own conversion, I regard
myself as being particularly fortunate. A friend of my
father's heard that I had recently come to faith in Christ.
He was an elder in a church on the other side of town. He
phoned and invited me for a coffee. We chatted and
agreed to meet again. Over the next year he made himself
available. He shared his own prayer life and his love of
Scripture, he encouraged me to share doubts and ask
questions. Throughout that early time, which was a time
of great enthusiasm and confusion, he was always
available. Then throughout my ministry I would get the
odd call, the word of encouragement.

God provided for me; however, it did not come
because some church had a scheme in place. How many
disciples never follow far because we have not taken the
time to give them someone who will help point out a few
of the potholes on the way!

Short interval
- Who could value from hearing your testimony and personal experience of God?

Evangelism

In and out evangelism

'Out: evangelism as sales pitch, as conquest, as warfare, as ultimatum, as threat, as argument, as entertainment, as show, as monologue, as something you have to do.

In: discipleship-making as conversation, as friendship, as influence, as invitation, as challenge, as opportunity, as conversation, as dance, as something you have got to do.'[61]

So writes Brian McLaren. McLaren is helpfully pointing out that a paradigm shift needs to take place with regard to how the church reaches people with the good news of Jesus. While our motives can be prompted by love, still our evangelism has appeared to be a well-thought-out manoeuvre ready to be unleashed upon the unsuspecting non-faith community. Our desire is to reconnect people with God through the work of Jesus. However, our efforts are easy to caricature. Evangelism is mobilizing towards an event or a season. We have evangelistic campaigns and we celebrate the numbers of those who come forward responding to the call. The members of the congregation bring in an evangelist and at the end of a campaign are able to sit back and relax. The church has done its duty and tried to reach out. But has it?

Throughout this book I have been asserting that we must think again about how we are reaching into the fast-changing western world. While we have already thought about some of the ways in which we can do this, in this section I want us to reflect upon three: the changing relationships within society, the lack of knowledge about faith issues and God's missional plan. The rest of the section provides further illustration of how these come together in Scripture and the church.

Hey that's my song

When I first started listening to music I remember the joy of going to a record store, picking out an album and bringing it home. Then, after looking at the cover, I would wait until everyone was out before I could listen. We only had one turntable in the house, so there was always a fight to see who got there first! I remember the joy of getting a portable cassette recorder and being able to listen to my music in my own space and at my own time, although not always at my preferred volume.

Now I have an MP3 player. I download individual tracks from the internet and make up my own personal soundtracks. No one else will have the same selection in the same order as I do. I love the creativity of listening to clips from different artists, without having to buy a whole album. I can have jazz and blues, classical and gospel, and when I get fed up I simply put others on. Listening is no longer a community or social event but an individualistic experience, offering choice and variety that I alone can control.

When I take the underground in London I see lots of people listening or moving to the beat – each person listening to a different beat, disconnected from the other.

Perhaps there are twenty people responding to music all at the same time, in the same underground carriage, and yet there is no sense of belonging. This is the world in which we live. People demand the right to decide for themselves about what is important. What seemed right yesterday may still be right for you, but maybe not for me. Lives lack a sense of coherence. People shift from tradition to tradition whenever it suits. This fragmentation means that it is hard to find a centre or set of beliefs into which we can effectively communicate the gospel.

There are many positives to the way in which our societies are changing. The access to information is so much greater than before. The opportunity for creativity is much wider. The range of choice has never been greater. Looking at music and the arts is only a simple illustration of the speed of change that is taking place all around us. We could have used education or technology. Suddenly, things have become much more fluid than ever before. In the midst of this there is a lack of community. And it is in the context, as mentioned before, that we can share the gospel. We are compelled because we want to glorify God and also because we care passionately that people might experience community with God and with his people. And we are compelled to think how best we can reach these people.

No idea what you're talking about

On several occasions I have been asked to take a funeral for someone from the wider community and encountered a total lack of knowledge about Jesus and the message. One particular example stays with me.

The main point of contact for the funeral was in her fifties and had never been involved in church. The daughter, probably in her thirties, had never been to church since childhood. Her own daughter was in her mid-teens and, apart from religious education classes and the occasional school assembly, had never heard about Christianity. While discussing the funeral service it became clear that this family did not know any hymns, nor did they know anything about what happened in a church. The real challenge for me was to listen without bombarding them with 'useful' information. Much of the normal faith language meant nothing to them. Here was a family who had no Bible, no prayer and no view about Jesus. Any thoughts that they did have were shaped by the media, particularly the tabloids. Yet the last remnants of Christendom still remain. These people still wanted a Christian service, although they did not actually know what that meant.

This is not an isolated incident. Many other ministers could tell similar stories. So what should be done? I believe it is a poor gospel witness not to think about what we are saying, how we say it and to whom. Things that would be clear to those with a church background no longer make any sense to those in our communities. I am not advocating that we change what it is we believe, or even the heart of the message. However, we do need to try and put ourselves into the minds of those who have never heard. What do they understand by what we are doing and saying? What does it say to the wider community when we have made no attempt to listen and dialogue with those around us?

We could learn much from those who have gone overseas to serve God. They spend countless hours learning the language and thinking about the culture that they are going into. They will read and learn and ask questions because eventually they will have to live in a different environment where people will be watching how they fit in. It is a long-term commitment, but to be an authentic witness time has to be spent understanding those who God has called them to serve and live amongst.

The western world is a mission field for the church. To be good news people will take commitment. We will have to learn to function in ways that seem strange to us. A lot of time will be required in listening and reflecting so that we can effectively communicate the good news in ways that make sense.

Where did they go?

God is a God of mission. The plan to redeem and bring healing to a lost and broken world flows from the heart of God. The mission belongs to God. Throughout time God has been active and powerful in the ways in which he has brought about his saving purposes. Throughout the records of Scripture we are given a picture of the God who is active in reaching out. The God who made promises to Abraham is also the one who led the people. The God who formed a people to be his own is the same one who called the prophets to proclaim both his love and his judgement. Ultimately, the full expression of that missional heart is revealed to us in the life, death, resurrection and ascension of Jesus Christ, and in the sending of the Holy Spirit to empower the church to be his witnesses.

The high or central point of God's missional plan and activity is found in Jesus Christ: the Word who became flesh and dwelt among us. The Son of God who came to die on the cross was touched and touchable. He knew and could be known. We could use the term incarnational to describe the mission of God in Christ. At the heart of the Christian message is the wonder of grace found in the fact that God came into the world.

> It is the word that was in the beginning, that was with God and that was God that becomes flesh and graciously enables his creatures to behold his glory, full of grace and truth. That this word becomes flesh is an event of divine grace. The way that the incarnate word becomes visible, audible and knowable in the life, death and resurrection of Jesus Christ reveals the majestic and sovereign grace of God accomplishing God's purposes within human history.[62]

I believe that we need to think afresh about incarnation as the paradigm for mission. By this I am not in any way seeking a reductionist view of evangelism or the gospel. Of course we must be pointing people to the cross of Christ and we should be able to give an account for why we believe what we do. However, we must be doing that in the context of being touchable and knowable. There is an incident in the life of Jesus that highlights the point that I am trying to stress. The story is recorded in the Gospel of Mark.

The gift of touch

A man with leprosy comes to Jesus and begs him to make him clean (Mk. 1:40-45). The leper believes that if Jesus is willing then he can be healed. In the mind of the leper there is no doubt about the power of Jesus but there are doubts about whether Jesus would be willing to use that power for someone like him. As we read this passage we see that Jesus reaches out his hand. The Son of God reaches out his hand to a leper and touches him.

Why did Jesus choose to heal this man through touch? He could have done it simply by speaking. It may have been that as compassion gripped the heart of Jesus, he wanted to identify with this man. Perhaps too it was so that the man could more fully grasp the wonder of God's willingness to bring healing. I wonder when this man had last felt the touch of kindness and love upon him.

I am convinced that the memory of the healing of the leper would have stayed with the disciples. Their master, who, appearing to them after the resurrection, would tell them to put their fingers in his hands, used those same hands to touch a leper. After the Great Commission they would be challenged by the fact that the Word that had become flesh actually used that flesh to bring healing and wholeness to those who were at the very margins of society. Jesus entered right into the heart of the suffering and misery of the culture into which he was born. This is the depths of the grace of God in the incarnation. God entered into the pain to bring transformation. It was not just the words of Jesus that made a difference but also his presence. The acts of grace in a graceless world drew people to praise God. Attitudes were changed and situations were transformed because of the incarnational presence of God.

Reprise
Don't just stand there – do something!

Jesus called people to follow him. He also encouraged them to come to him if they were heavy-laden and world-weary. However, Jesus was primarily a sender. Whether it was the twelve disciples, or the group of seventy-two or all the disciples post-resurrection, the model was the same. They were told to go. The man with the legion of demons is told to go back home and tell how much God had done for him (Lk. 8:39). The disciples were sent out and told to go from house to house and village to village, not taking much with them. If the response was poor they were to kick the dust from their feet and move on to another community (Lk. 10:5-12). They were not to stand around and wait on people coming to them, rather they were to live and speak with those whom they meet.

The disciples were being taught how to incarnate the message. The message becomes flesh in that they go and spend time in communities. They preach, heal and live among people. They are being forced to build bridges with those outside of the faith community. In the great commission given by Jesus to the disciples he tells them to go and make disciples of all nations. Again, the emphasis is upon going and transforming. The very nature of disciple-making will change both the individuals and those around them, bringing transformation. The disciples are not to think only of Jerusalem, hoping that others will join them; they must go into different culture settings and societies. They will have to trust in Christ and live out that faith in the midst of a multicultural world.

Jesus was continually sending. Some were to go back to where they had been while others went from village to village, and even to the ends of the earth. Yet is it not true that much of our evangelism has not been based on waiting and bringing rather than going or sending? We develop campaigns and courses that are designed to bring people to us. Much of the drive is often how we will get our numbers to increase at our main worship gathering. At the heart of what we are doing is how we can get others to come to us rather than how we can go to them.

I have led leadership conferences and I have asked the leaders some basic questions about the people who live within a couple of miles of the church buildings: the percentage breakdown of different age groups and what people do. I enquire about the real issues that are faced by those who live within that community. At first I was surprised by how little some churches seemed to know. However, after more discussion what became clear was that churches were running courses from their building but actually had little presence within the community. Their motives were correct – they desired to see people united with Jesus – but they wanted people to come to them to find out about faith. In fact many leaders did not live in or around the place where they worshipped. The model seemed to be a proclamation on our terms rather than a long-term commitment to preach, heal and touch the society all around us.

Perhaps we have become frightened of the culture outside our faith communities and have become engrossed in maintaining church structures. Whatever the reason, we have lost the desire to evangelise incarnationally. Rather than being risky senders we have lost the passion to interact in meaningful ways with those we are called to love and serve. Communities are not being transformed because we are not involved in them, bringing honesty and hope. We have to stop looking for the quick fix, pain-free 'come and hear evangelism', and discover a long-term commitment to being there.

I wonder how often we, as a church, come into contact with the lepers of our communities. To meet them we would have to be in the streets where they are. Our presence would need to be recognized by others and we would have to be prepared to stop and enter into a dialogue that may lead to a relationship which is worthwhile in itself. Part of the call to incarnational living is to see the value of friendships with others; to show a genuine delight and interest in meeting new friends, recognizing that they are precious to God.

There is excitement in the possibility of what God may say to us or do in us through others who are not part of the faith community – to see people not just as numbers to be won or souls to be saved but lives to be shared, and a genuine desire to get to know them. For the church to think in this way does not mean that it is in some way denying the good news of Jesus. Nor does it indicate that there is now little confidence in the proclamation of the Word of God. Rather, it is a call to whole-life evangelism, where we take seriously the need to live out what we say. It is a cry to stop compartmentalizing evangelism as something that we do from time to time and make it something we are involved in minute by minute as good news people.

Short interval

- Think about who you come into contact with on a daily basis. Are there missed opportunities that you could make more of?

- Do those around you see and know that you are a Christian by your words and actions?

- Are you reaching out like Jesus and the disciples did? If not, why not?

Without the bridge you fall into the water

The church in the western world is in numerical decline. I have tried to show some of the effects of this as it impacts the way in which we think about evangelism. Indeed, I would go further and say that some of the ways in which we have gone about evangelising have contributed to the church's decline. Many have little connection with a faith community. They are mistrusting of an institution which proclaims absolutes in an arrogant and condescending manner. Where once we could have whispered and been heard now we need a megaphone.

So what should we do? How should we react? As mentioned before, we need to respond by engaging creatively and consistently with the world as incarnational people. However that does not mean that the church should be discouraged or frightened by what is happening. We need to re-evaluate what we have been doing. This is part of the continual reformation of the church. It is the call to the excitement of what God is doing and to jump on board with it. Evaluation can be painful, and it could lead to new ways that at first we are uncomfortable with.

For example, a revolution of praxis may be required if we are to remain faithful to our calling and live lives that glorify Jesus Christ as Saviour and Lord. So, rather than having breakfasts or lunches at the church, we could invite members to make breakfast for their neighbours or have a buffet for friends and workmates; acts of love that model community in a world where real community is difficult to find. In this way we are making ourselves and our faith accessible.

Robert Webber maintains that 'Social networking in a postmodern world will primarily happen where people eat together in the homes of Christians and in neighbourhood communities where faith may be shared.'[63] He also notes that in the early church there were two important themes around hospitality: 'Christians must recognize themselves as strangers in the world. Also . . . Christians must recognize strangers as Christ.'[64] While that may sound a little programmatic I think that the important point is that through acts of generosity and kindness we can create models of community within our wider social settings. To regard every stranger as Christ might radically alter the way in which we viewed our mission and encourage us to focus more on sharing with the stranger than we may have done in the past.

To transform the world we will need to place our missional energies in different ways. Rather than calling people to come to us we must be equipping people to live out the gospel in the world. This may mean that we give people more space to get involved in non-church activities. Sometimes we have members of the Christian community spending every available minute 'doing' church rather than living faith: teaching children, sitting on committees, delivering magazines. Sometimes it is the same group of committed people who are doing all of these. By the time that our members are finished doing all the church work they have no time to relax and make friends in the wider community. It takes time to develop real and fruitful relationships. Being part of the community does not just happen. You have to have a commitment to be around others. To go to the movies with neighbours or to join a school board – it is about making the time to be involved. For that to happen, the church itself must be encouraging people to see that spending time making friends and being around their communities is not wasted time but is part of the call to follow Jesus.

Living out faith in the midst of people who have never considered that Jesus may make a difference to them will not be easy, but it is part of the incarnational witness of the church. It is what we are called to. It may mean that we have to structure church life in such a way that meetings and some activities close down so that relationships can grow. This won't be easy for some of us to accept. We judge our success as a church by the numbers that are attending our meetings. The only growth indicator that we tend to be interested in is growth in attendance. Can it be that we can be successful by being less concerned with numbers but more concerned with our engagement in the world? We may have to ask whether our prime goal is numbers or about the Kingdom of God advancing.

One of the main places of connection for us with those outside the church is found in our workplace.[65] While it is true that more people are working alone or from home than before, many of us still go into an office, or sit in a staff room. It can be hard to be upfront about our faith within a work environment. Sometimes we might be the only Christian presence and we can feel under the spotlight. It is easy to be intimidated and feel that people will have a negative view of us when they find out about our commitment to Jesus. Nobody wants to feel that they are an outsider.

It is normal to want to fit in. Sometimes the temptation is either to be like everyone else, hiding who we are, or to keep ourselves separate from what is happening around us. But we should see work as a calling. God has put us within that work place at this particular time so that we can be channels of his grace. If he has called us then he will be with us. It is important that we are confident enough to be ourselves; to accept that while we are not yet perfect we are a work under construction, and that we can live faithfully believing that God is at work. It is the authentic day-to-day living among others that will make an impact in the world. It is sharing who we are in the world that makes a difference.

This is not about delivering proof texts or even friendship evangelism (by this I mean regarding friendship as a means to an end), it is living lovingly and honestly in the world. By this consistent, prayerful

witness we are building bridges in the places God has
called us to be. One Christian living authentically in the
workplace may be influencing more people in a day than
church leaders like me in a whole week. The workplace is
a vital part of the engagement between Christians and
wider social groupings. By simply living for Christ with
honesty and integrity we are pointing others to the
mystery of faith and the possibilities of life experience
that has so far been beyond their understanding. God
may be using our lives to break down generations of
ignorance and suspicion. Through the relationships that
are made we may find that friends and workmates begin
to ask questions about what is important to us. Faith
conversations may happen naturally as we build respect
and people learn to trust who we are. We need to be
ourselves, breaking down the stereotypes and believing
that God is able to use the simple witness of his people to
extend the Kingdom of God.

Some may think that I am advocating a watering down
of the gospel, but that is not the case. I am advocating that
we live a radical Christian life fully devoted to Jesus
as Lord. However, we live this life in the world rather
than the church. We live it in the midst of the struggles
and pains of those all around us. By living in a way that
is radical in love and grace God may use that life to
help transform society. Conversations will not need to
be forced, nor friendships manipulated – things happen
naturally (or supernaturally) because we are a living
presence of the gospel. This will take a rethink about
priorities for the church. It will also be a challenge to us
as individuals. We would have to ask whether our
lifestyle actually does allow people to see something of
the grace of God. As neighbours or workmates engage
with us over time will they see a radical edge to our
lives? Will our priorities and our kindness provoke

discussion among others? Could we get to the stage where people are thinking, or even saying it is good to have a Christian on the staff? Or will neighbours be glad because of the changes in the community that are taking place through Christian acts of love from those who live there?

High-pitched adventure

I want to illustrate the idea of incarnational mission by introducing you to two people who have lived out their faith among young people with little or no connection with any faith group. I am sure that these stories could be replicated in many places; I have included them to encourage and challenge you.

Julie

Julie was a young married woman who had a heart for young people. She was appointed as youth worker at Perth Riverside Church. The church was new and did not have a church building; worship took place in the local primary school.

The wider community was a mixed one. There were various social difficulties affecting various parts of the area. There were many teenagers hanging around the streets with little to do.

Rather than go out with some plan or programme in mind, Julie decided after a lot of prayer, to walk round the area and see what was really happening. It didn't take long to find some kids looking for things to do. What took much longer was gaining trust and building relationships. She would keep going, talking and primarily listening to what the young people had to say. It was a journey of mutual discovery. Julie learned more about the community and their aspirations and problems

while they began to discover someone who had a care
and commitment to them.

Over a longer period Julie became the trusted friend
and support for many of the young people. She was
someone who lived out her faith among them and they
respected her. It was not always easy. Some young people
were wrestling with really difficult problems. There were
issues of self-worth, anger, frustration, family problems,
and a whole lot of other things that couldn't be worked
through in a day; things that needed consistency and
availability.

Julie would talk to other agencies, liaise with schools
and look to find ways of helping young people to find a
better future. All this took its toll: getting texts all the
time, late night phone calls, trying to walk with people as
they faced one problem after another. Sometimes it was
hugely frustrating, as teenagers fell into the same traps
again and again. However, there were others who really
moved on in life. Many gained confidence and found
new possibilities for their future.

There were also conversations about faith. Many of the
youngsters knew nothing about Jesus but there was an
interest and openness about spiritual things. Questions
were being asked and discussions taking place about the
good news of Jesus, and how knowing him could radically change life for ever. Over several years many of these
young people came to a knowledge of Jesus as Saviour
and Lord.

The step of faith was difficult enough for some, and
following Jesus as a disciple was going to be incredibly
difficult. Trusting Jesus didn't mean that suddenly all
life's problems were going to vanish, and for many there
were struggles about continuing to follow Jesus. But the
wonderful thing is that the grace of God has been seen
over and over again in these lives as they began to

discover that life is different from how they thought it should be. In Jesus there were endless possibilities of what life might be like. They were able to understand more fully ideas of worth and status. They also experienced the care of a committed Christian who wanted the best for them. Whether they came to faith or not, they all benefited from the fact that Julie had gone out looking to meet young people with a view to building meaningful relationships. A love for Christ and for those within the community compelled her to take risks of faith to build friendships that made a difference.

John
The same could be said of a young man from Glasgow who came to work as a volunteer at our church for a year before taking up a place at Bible College. John Craig came and lived right in the heart of the parish. While I never heard John preach the gospel, I saw him seek to live it out, and recognized the impact that it made upon others. John would turn up at houses for coffee and stay and chat for hours. He would go to concerts with young folk, spend time laughing, chatting about music or sport, or if the chance was there he would talk about Jesus. John had a natural ability to make friends and get alongside others, no matter what their background was. He was the same whether he was in church or out, and gradually that authentic living started to make an impact upon others. I am convinced that through the commitment of both these young Christians there were many whose view of Christians, faith, and even the church has been altered for ever.

In order for that to happen there had to be a long-term sacrificial engagement with people. It meant time, energy and sometimes huge disappointment and frustration. It was born out of a desire to take the love of Jesus out of the church and into the world. It was in the long-term incarnational ministry that enabled a group of non-churched the chance to discover who Jesus is. This is being done by many people in lots of ways around the country and it is very exciting. These were people who would not have come to the church but were reached as the church was mobilized to live faith in the world. In a society were social bonding is in decline and previous ties no longer hold, it is vital that Christians make meaningful relationships in the world. The world will be transformed as Christ is seen in a million homes and work places, when the church lives out its message at the heart of communities.

Reprise

It is wonderful when the saving grace of God in Christ touches any life. We should celebrate whatever way in which God works, and I am not criticising what churches do. However, we need to respond to a fast-changing society. The western nations are our mission field and we need to re-evaluate the way in which we view evangelism. The Jesus model of incarnational sending is the one that I believe is the most helpful within our current situation: acknowledging and engaging with the cultures in which we live. We need to listen and share our lives with others. Imagine if Christians were making a contribution to every neighbourhood where they were placed, and building friendships all over the place. Think of the kingdom possibilities as people encounter people who love Jesus and love others. What would happen if Christians were getting involved in every area of life just because it was the right thing to do?

After being interviewed at a church a woman came up to speak to me. 'I really love jazz,' she said. She had the gleam in her eye of the real enthusiast. 'My favourite is Duke Ellington,' she continued. 'He didn't just write music and get people to play you know. He would listen to the musicians play a few pieces then he would write music that they were comfortable with and could interpret. It takes a great person to listen.'

I have not been able to find out if what the lady said was correct, but I hope it was. I really love the picture of a great composer taking the time to listen to musicians and keeping them in mind as he writes. It would be a wonderful fusion of his talent and creative vision with their journey and abilities. It would be a mixture of listening and dialogue, creating something greater than any of the separate parts. I believe we are called to listen and dialogue, getting involved in the world so that something wonderful happens that is greater than any of the individual parts. This would be good news to the world.

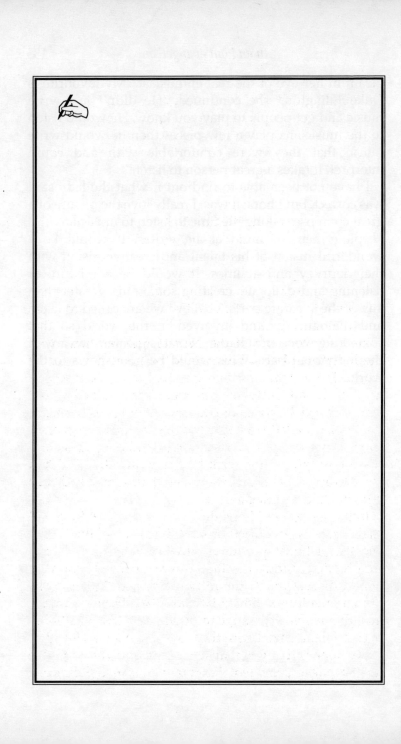

Conclusion

'Well, what did you think of the concert?'

'I love that swing stuff, and some of the solos were great,' Caroline replied.

We had come out of the concert hall and went to a small Italian place where we talked over a couple of lattes. From that starting question the conversation headed in all sorts of directions. We talked about favourite artists, styles of jazz and other types of music. The topics spilled over into the role of music in society, even music therapy. It was fun, articulating ideas and sharing insights. Time went by really quickly. We didn't come to any conclusions; it was the sharing that had been both fun and a challenge.

In the same way I hope this book will be uplifting and challenging. The subjects around the future of the church and its relationship with culture are huge ones. I have simply tried to add a few thoughts to the mix. I believe an honest discussion on the response of the church to the changing cultural climate is vital. That discussion must include the role of creative improvisation and an attitude of risky engagement with the world that God so loved.

My hope is that you may take some notes and scribble on the pages provided. Perhaps you can reflect upon some of the themes and track down some of the books in the bibliography. I do not think that there are any clear answers to some of the issues raised. However, my desire is that as we dialogue we will find that the exploration is worth it. And maybe we will be able to live the kingdom tune with real style, providing transformation both to the church and the world.

Key notes

1 Plutarch.
2 Meaningless because society has changed and become more fluid, and so the church needs to respond to this.
3 See *Leadership Jazz* (Dell Publishing, 1992).
4 Lesslie Newbigin, *The Gospel in a Pluralist Society* (Eerdmans, 2000), p.227, emphasis added.
5 Darrell L. Guder, *The Incarnation and the Church's Witness* (Trinity Press, 2000), p.22.
6 Douglas John Hall, *The End of Christendom and the Future of Christianity* (Trinity Press, 1995), p.1.
7 See the Edict of Milan. Later work was carried on by Theodosius 1.
8 Rodney Clapp, *A Peculiar People* (IVP, 1996), p.25. Clapp has a very helpful discussion about the negative effects of Constantinianism in his section 'The Church as Unchurched – How Christians became useless'.
9 Ibid.
10 Douglas John Hall, *The End of Christendom and the Future of Christianity*, pp.7-8. Hall's view is that the church is finding it hard to make a creative response to its changing situation because of an inbuilt commitment to established institutional models.
11 Callum G. Brown, *The Death of Christian Britain* (Routledge Press, 2000), p.1. Brown analyzes the formulations of religion and secularization and plots reasons for decline of organized religion.
12 Eddie Gibbs and Ian Coffey, *Church Next* (IVP, 2001), p.21.
13 Gerald A. Arbuckle, *Grieving for Change* (Geoffrey Chapman, 1991), p.3.
14 Ibid. Arbuckle contends that the church has to go through a grieving process before it can move on to the place that God is calling it to.
15 Lesslie Newbigin, *The Gospel in a Pluralist Society*, p.14.
16 David J. Williams, *Acts* (NIBC Hendrickson, 1990), p.303. Williams' commentary throws helpful insights concerning Paul's communication of the gospel in a pluralist society.

17 Pete Ward, *Selling Worship* (Paternoster Press, 2004), pp.102-103. Ward helpfully shows the way in which Christian worship styles have altered; often as a response to a changing culture.

18 Gilbert Harman, 'Is There a Single True Morality?' in *Moral Relativism – A Reader*, ed. Paul K. Moser and Thomas L. Carson (Oxford University Press, 2000), p.165.

19 Gordon Graham, 'Tolerance, Pluralism and Relativism' in *Moral Relativism – A Reader*, ed. Paul K. Moser and Thomas L. Carson, p.229.

20 Jonathan R. Wilson, *Living Faithfully in a Fragmented World* (Trinity Press, 1997), p.27. Wilson reflects upon the work of Alistair McIntyre's *After Virtue*, drawing lessons for the church. He seeks to analyze the life of the church in our culture.

21 Victor Turner, *On the Edge of the Bush: Anthropology as Experience* (University Arizona Press, 1986).

22 Scholars of Atlanta Georgia, *Victor Turner Revisited* (American Academy of Religion, 1991), p.42.

23 Alan J. Roxburgh, *Missionary Congregation, Leadership, and Liminality* (Trinity Press, 1997), p.23.

24 Ibid p.32.

25 Walter Brueggemann, *Cadences of Home* (Westminster John Knox Press, 1997), p.42.

26 Walter Brueggemann, *The Prophetic Imagination* (Fortress Press, 2001), p.4.

27 Dirk Sutro, *Jazz for Dummies* (IOG Books, 1998), p.19.

28 See Louis Armstrong, *In His Own Words* (Oxford University Press, 1991), p.11. *In His Own Words* shows that Armstrong's music flowed from the cultural dynamic and uncertainty that was shaping the nation. His music is a product of these changes.

29 Jerry Coker, *Improving Jazz* (Simon & Schuster, 1964), p.9. The introduction by Schuller is a helpful reflection on the place of thinking through possibilities as part of the process of improvisation.

30 Leonard Sweet, *Summoned to Lead* (Zondervan, 2004), p.55.

31 Ibid p.68.

32 Michael H. Zack, *Organization Science* (Vol. 11, no. 2, April 2000), p.232. Zack discusses jazz organization and improvisation as a model for business. He compares music with conversation; particularly interactive conversation with jazz. He concludes that successful business leaders will require models involving much more dynamism and flexibility.

33 Ibid p.231.

34 Ted Giola, *The History of Jazz* (Oxford University Press, 1997), p.9.

35 Max De Pree, *Leadership Jazz*, p.181.

36 Leonard Sweet, *Soul Salsa* (Zondervan, 2000), p.146.

37 Eugene H. Peterson, *Life at its Best* (Zondervan, 2002), p.388. This trilogy combines *The Gift*, *The Journey* and *The Quest* in one volume.

38 Lesslie Newbigin, *Proper Confidence: Faith, Doubt and Certainty in Christian Discipleship* (Eerdmans, 1995), p.105.

39 John R.W. Stott, *The Message of Acts* (IVP, 1994), p.82.

40 Robert E. Webber, *Ancient – Future Evangelism* (Baker, 2003), p.115.

41 Rodney Clapp, *A Peculiar People* (IVP, 1996), p.95.

42 See www.cmgworldwide.com/music/Holiday. Accessed January 2006.

43 Parker J. Palmer, *The Courage to Teach* (Jossey-Bass, 1998), p.27.

44 'U2 Eucharist radicalising the faithful' in *The Scotsman*, 4th April 2006.

45 Louis J. Luzbetak, *The Church and Cultures* (Orbis Books, 1989), p.296.

46 Robert E. Webber, *Ancient – Future Evangelism*, pp.63-64.

47 Alan Jamieson, *A Churchless Faith* (SPCK, 2002), pp.60-74. While more research has now been done concerning the faith journeys, this work is however extremely thought-provoking with regard to what might be the church's response to the growing numbers keeping faith but leaving church.

48 Walter Brueggemann, *Cadences of Home*, p.42.

49 David Watson, *Discipleship* (Hodder & Stoughton, 1983) .

50 Ken Gire, *The Divine Embrace* (Tyndale House, 2004), p.7.

51 Sting, 'Englishman in New York'.

52 Derek Kidner, *Genesis* (Tyndale OT Commentaries, IVP, 1981), p.171.

53 *Time* Magazine, Special 100 Edition.

54 Darrell L. Bock, *Luke* (NT Commentary Series, IVP, 1994), p.300.

55 Karl Barth, *The Call to Discipleship* (Fortress Press, 1958), p.13.

56 Dietrich Bonhoeffer, *The Cost of Discipleship* (Simon & Schuster, 1959), p.88 .

57 *Book of Common Order of the Church of Scotland* (Saint Andrew Press, 1994), p.2.

58 By modernist church expectations I am meaning expectations that we place upon new disciples that refer more to the culture that has pervaded the church rather than biblical faith itself.

59 Eugene H. Peterson, *A Long Obedience in the Same Direction* (IVP, 1980), p.27. This is a reflection on discipleship Psalms 120-134, showing discipleship as a pilgrimage.

60 John Swinton, *Resurrecting the Person* (Abingdon Press, 2000), p.162. John challenges models of control and power that have often marked the church's engagement with the world.

61 Brian D. McLaren, *More Ready Than You Realize* (Zondervan, 2002). (Back cover quote from author) The conversation that takes place throughout the book illuminates spiritual friendship and the patience and joy found in deepening, questioning relationships.

62 Darrell L. Guder, *The Incarnation and the Church's Witness* (Trinity Press, 1999), p.4. Guder helpfully shows that the conversion of the church will happen as it embraces more fully the incarnation mission of Christ.

63 Robert E. Webber, *Ancient – Future Evangelism*, p.58.

64 Ibid p.55. This is a very helpful look at Christian formation and its application in a postmodern world.

65 I have found the work of Mark Greene very helpful in the area of Christians in the workplace. For further information on his work with the London Institute for Contemporary Christianity visit www.licc.org.uk. The bibliography also lists his book on work.

Bibliography

Books

Alexander, Bobby Chris, *Victor Turner Revisited* (University of Arizona, 1985)

Arbuckle, Gerald A., *Grieving for Change* (Geoffrey Chapman, 1991)

Armstrong, Louis, *In His Own Words* (Oxford University Press, 1991)

Barth, Karl, *The Call to Discipleship* (Fortress Press, 1958)

Bock, Darrell L., *Luke* (NT Commentary Series, IVP, 1994)

Bonhoeffer, Dietrich, *The Cost of Discipleship* (Simon & Schuster, 1959)

Brown, Callum G., *The Death of Christian Britain* (Routledge Press, 2000)

Brueggemann, Walter, *Cadences of Home* (Westminster John Knox Press, 1997)

Brueggemann, Walter, *The Prophetic Imagination* (Fortress Press, 2001)

Carson, Donald, *The Gospel According to John* (IVP, 1991)

Clapp, Rodney, *A Peculiar People* (IVP, 1996)

Coker, Jerry, *Improving Jazz* (Simon & Schuster, 1964)

De Pree, Max, *Leadership Jazz* (Dell Publishing, 1992)

Ferguson, Niall, *Empire* (Penguin Books Ltd., 2003)

Gibbs, Eddie and Ian Coffey, *Church Next* (IVP, 2001)

144   *Bibliography*

Giola, Ted, *The History of Jazz* (Oxford University Press, 1997)

Gire, Ken, *The Divine Embrace* (Tynedale House, 2004)

Gooding, David, *According to Luke* (IVP, 1987)

Greene, Mark, *Thank God it's Monday* (Scripture Union, 2001)

Guder, Darrell L., *The Continuing Conversion of the Church* (Eerdmans, 2000)

Guder, Darrell L., *The Incarnation and the Church's Witness* (Trinity Press, 2000)

Hall, Douglas John, *The End of Christendom and the Future of Christianity* (Trinity Press, 1995)

Jamieson, Alan, *A Churchless Faith* (SPCK, 2002)

Kidner, Derek, *Genesis* (Tyndale OT Commentaries, IVP, 1981)

Luzbetak, Louis J., *The Church and Cultures* (Orbis Books, 1989)

McLaren, Brian D., *A New Kind of Christian* (Jossey-Bass, 2001)

McLaren, Brian D., *More Ready Than You Realize* (Zondervan, 2002)

Moser, Paul K. and Thomas L. Carson, *Moral Relativism – A Reader* (Oxford University Press, 2000)

Newbigin, Lesslie, *Proper Confidence: Faith, Doubt and Certainty in Christian Discipleship* (Eerdmans, 1995)

Newbigin, Lesslie, *The Gospel in a Pluralist Society* (Eerdmans, 2000)

Peterson, Eugene H., *A Long Obedience in the Same Direction* (IVP, 2000)

Peterson, Eugene H., *Life at its Best* (Zondervan, 2002)

Palmer, Parker J., *The Courage to Teach* (Jossey-Bass, 1998)

Roxburgh, Alan J., *Missionary Congregation, Leadership, and Liminality* (Trinity Press, 1997)

Scholars of Atlanta Georgia, *Victor Turner Revisited*, (American Academy of Religion, 1991)

Stott, John R.W., *The Message of Acts* (IVP, 1994)

Sutro, Dirk, *Jazz for Dummies* (IOG Books, 1998)

Sweet, Leonard, *Soul Salsa* (Zondervan, 2000)

Sweet, Leonard, *Summoned to Lead* (Zondervan, 2004)

Swinton, John, *Resurrecting the Person* (Abingdon Press, 2000)

Thurston, Bonnie Bowman, *Spiritual Life in the Early Church* (Fortress Press, 1993)

Tolerance, Gordon Graham, *Pluralism and Relativism*

Turner, Victor, *On the Edge of the Bush: Anthropology as Experience* (University Arizona Press, 1986)

Ward, Pete, *Selling Worship* (Paternoster Press, 2004)

Watson, David, *Discipleship* (Hodder & Stoughton, 1983)

Webber, Robert E., *Ancient – Future Evangelism* (Baker, 2003)

Williams, David J., *Acts* (NIBC Hendrickson, 1990)

Wilson, Jonathan R., *Living Faithfully in a Fragmented World* (Trinity Press, 1997)

Zack, Michael, *Organization Science* (Vol. 11, no. 2, April 2000)